# Ulys

# The War Years

**By Michael W. Simmons**

# Table of Contents

# Chapter One: Lieutenant Sam Grant

## From Point Pleasant to West Point

Ulysses S. Grant, the eighteenth president of the United States, was born on April 27, 1822, in Point Pleasant, Ohio. On both sides of his family, he was descended from British settlers who had arrived in the New World before the Revolutionary War. Grant's father Jesse came of a family which had resided in America for eight generations by the time of his eldest son's birth; in the 1600s, his ancestor Matthew Grant had been amongst the original settlers of the Massachusetts Bay Colony. His mother Hannah's Scottish ancestors had arrived in the British American colonies about forty years prior to American independence, and both his maternal and paternal ancestors had fought in Washington's army against the British.

Grant's family had joined the American trend of westward expansion after the Revolutionary war, crossing the Appalachian Mountains through Kentucky to settle in Ohio. Though he was born in Point Pleasant, he lived there only a year before his father resettled in nearby Georgetown, a community of approximately the same size as Point Pleasant, but with more promising business prospects for Jesse's tannery business. Grant was the first-born child of his parents but he would later have five siblings, including three sisters and two brothers.

As a boy, Ulysses had a patchy education, migrating from the one room schoolhouse in Georgetown to two separate one-year stints at boarding schools in Kentucky and Ohio. A self-professed indifferent scholar, Grant would later reflect that he "probably did not make progress enough to compensate for the outlay in board and tuition." Though he demonstrated no outstanding academic talents, he did possess one unique ability which won him fame in his community; he was a prodigiously gifted horseman. "Horses seem to understand Ulysses," his mother once commented, after concerned neighbors saw her young son swinging on a horse's tail, a liberty which horses did not normally allow small humans to take without rewarding them with a swift kick.

By the time Grant was eight, he was a capable enough driver that he could haul the wagonloads of wood that his father's tannery needed in order to operate (although he was still too small to load and unload the wood himself—the adult men had to assist him there.) When he was eleven, he took upon himself the responsibility for plowing his family's fields. "From that age until seventeen, I did all the work with the horses," Grant would later write. Rather than regarding such responsibilities as an unduly burdensome chore, Grant reveled in the freedom it granted him. Seemingly recognizing that their son was upholding an adult's responsibilities on the farm, his parents likewise allowed him an adult's discretion regarding how to spend his spare time, whether it was swimming in the pond in the summer or hitching up the wagon and traveling to the next county to visit his grandparents for an afternoon.

Grant's responsibilities around the family farm had to be given up, however, after his father decided to send him to West Point as a teenager. Grant was not especially enthused by the prospect at first, but his father persuaded him. By going to West Point, he would have access to one of the best educational opportunities available in the United States in the 1840s. Though West Point was a military institution, the majority of its graduates did not go on lifetime careers in the military. Jesse's wish was that Ulysses should study engineering. There was an urgent need for engineers due to American expansion into the western frontier, and West

Point was one of only two institutions in the nation that then offered engineering courses. From Jesse Grant's point of view, his eldest son could not do better than to gain training in such a lucrative career, at no expensive to himself or his family, since West Point tuition was paid for by the government.

Applicants to West Point required recommendations to be admitted, usually from a member of Congress. As it happened, Jesse Grant was well acquainted with a Congressman named Thomas Hamer; they had been friends once, only to split acrimoniously over a difference of political opinion. Both men had come to regret the rupture however, so when Jesse Grant submitted a humble petition that Hamer give Ulysses his recommendation, Hamer granted the favor immediately and chided Jesse for not having written sooner.

It was Thomas Haber who became responsible for bestowing upon Ulysses S. Grant the name by which he would become known to history. His father had chosen the name Hiram, while his maternal grandmother, a fan of classic Greek mythology, had chosen Ulysses. Haber, who had never met Jesse Grant's son, mistakenly recorded his name as Ulysses Grant when issuing the recommendation to West Point. He added the "S" as a middle initial because he knew that the boy's mother's maiden name was Simpson. As a result, Grant's name was added to the roster of West Point cadets as Ulysses S. Grant, and no amount of protesting on Grant's part could persuade anyone to change it.

Apart from the fact that attending West Point would send him east, thus enabling him to visit cities like Philadelphia and New York, which counted as metropolitan wonderlands to a boy who had grown up in what was technically frontier territory, Grant was no more enthusiastic about attending the military academy than he had been about attending boarding school. "When those two places [Philadelphia and New York] were visited," he later wrote, "I would have been glad to have had a steamboat or railroad collision, or any other accident happen, by which I might have received a temporary injury sufficient to make me ineligible...to enter the Academy. Nothing of the kind occurred, and I had to face the music."

Grant had been accustomed to a regular schedule of hard work since he was a young boy, so he managed to weather the grueling first year of training that new cadets at West Point are forced to undergo. The training which West Point cadets undertake today is little different from the training that cadets underwent when Grant first arrived in May of 1839. The bottom class was the largest and the senior class the smallest, because so many students washed out along the way. Grant had no love for the trappings of military discipline and military life, but he possessed an uncomplaining tenacity which enabled him to perform according to requirements. It was during his time at West Point that Grant acquired another name that was not quite his own. His fellow students called him Sam. It was the custom for cadets to bestow nicknames upon one another, nicknames that tended to follow them into the service after graduation. Upon seeing the name "U.S. Grant" posted on the roster list of new cadets, Grant's classmates seized upon the punning potential of his initials. "United States Grant" gave way to "Uncle Sam Grant", which was finally reduced to plain "Sam Grant".

Grant's friends and fellow students at West Point would have ample opportunity in later years to recollect their impressions of him as teenager. They would remember him as having been "fragile", possessed of "a girlish modesty; a hesitancy in presenting his own claims; a taciturnity born of his modesty; but a thoroughness in the accomplishment of whatever task was assigned to him... [He had] a noble, generous heart, a loveable character, and a sense of honor which was so perfect...that in the numerous cabals which were often formed his name was never mentioned." Physically, the young Grant was small and lithe, with a "delicate frame" which his friends blamed for his lack of enthusiasm for sports such as fencing and other military-themed forms of exercise; in fact, Grant simply disliked such exertions and avoided them when possible. But these aversions did not hurt his reputation amongst his classmates. "We all liked him," one of his fellow cadets remembered. "He had no bad habits."

Coming as he did from the uncultured vastness of the American frontier, Grant had a notable lack of social polish that was especially apparent in comparison to the scions of wealthy Southern families, who prided themselves on their sophistication and social talents. He was not especially devoted to his prescribed studies, but he discovered a passion for novel-reading: "There is a fine library connected with the Academy from which cadets can get books to read in their quarters," he would later write. "I devoted more time to these than to books relating to the course of studies. I read all of the works of Bulwer's then published, Cooper's, Marryat's, Scott's, Washington Irving's works, Lever's, and many others that I do not now remember." It is frequently the case that persons who become famous to history for their great accomplishments were indifferent students in the formal confines of classrooms, and shaped their own education by pursuing eclectic courses of self-selected reading. It was true of Washington, and so true of Lincoln as to be the cornerstone of the narrative of his early life. It was true of Grant as well.

Graduating West Point on any terms is no mean feat. All the same, Grant's standing was firmly in the middle of his class. Only in horsemanship did he excel, establishing a jump record that stood for twenty-five years after his departure. His scores and class ranking meant that Jesse Grant's hopes of an engineering career for his son were not to be realized; the engineering branch of the army took only the top graduates, while the combat branches took everyone else. But the notion of a career in the army had gradually come to appeal to Grant, and though he was disappointed when he was turned down for a cavalry posting on the grounds that there were no vacancies, he was pleased enough when his second choice was granted. Following a three-month furlough, Grant was posted to the 4th infantry at Jefferson Barracks, Missouri. He reported for duty in September 1843, when he was 21 years old.

## War and romance

Grant met the woman who would become his wife shortly after his graduation from West Point. One Grant's best friends at the academy was James Longstreet, the son of a wealthy, prominent Georgia family who would later become a high-ranking Confederate general. Like Grant, Longstreet was assigned to Jefferson Barracks. Like most young soldiers posted far from their homes, Grant and Longstreet missed the society and companionship of normal family life. As it happened, the family of Longstreet's West Point roommate, Fred Dent, lived in Missouri, not far from the Jefferson Barracks, and soon the Dent family were extending regular invitations to both young men. The Dents had a number of children, the youngest of which still lived at home, and Grant became extremely fond of the family—but he found additional incentive to spend time with them when their oldest daughter Julia returned home after completing her finishing school education and celebrating her debutante season. Where once Grant had found himself dining with the Dents one or two nights a week, he now found himself darkening their doorstep four or five nights of the week, whenever his duties permitted. Julia Dent was seventeen when first she met Grant. Esteemed by those who knew her as intelligent and well-informed for such a young girl, she was not thought to be a great beauty—she suffered from a congenital condition called strabismus which gave her a cross-eyed appearance—but she was widely admired all the same. Grant found her easy to talk to, and perhaps most importantly, she was an accomplished equestrienne who could easily keep pace with Grant's horsemanship.

Grant would later say that the outbreak of the Mexican-American War was chiefly responsible for making him understand the depth of his feelings for Julia, and for spurring him on to a proposal of marriage. As of 1843, Grant still did not see himself as having a long term career in the military. He had begun to aspire towards a career as a mathematics teacher at a school or university, and in order to gain the necessary experience, he had written to his old instructors at West Point to ask for a posting as an assistant professor there the following year. He was told that a place could be found for him, so he began to spend his spare time studying mathematics textbooks in his rooms in the evenings. Though he was beginning to have serious feelings for Julia Dent, he did not think, at first, that she returned them. At one point, prior to Grant's leaving Missouri on furlough to visit his family in Ohio, he had offered Julia his West Point class ring and asked her whether she might wear it. Julia later wrote that she misunderstood the intent behind his question, and had replied that she did not think her mother would approve of her accepting a gift of jewelry from a man. Grant accepted this rejection quietly, and did not press the issue.

Then, shortly before the outbreak of the Mexican-American War, Grant's regiment was ordered to Louisiana, in preparation for hostilities in Texas. The Republic of Texas had succeeded from Mexico in 1836 and declared its independence, and several major nations, including the United States, recognized Texan sovereignty, although Mexico did not. As far as Mexico was concerned, Texas was still the north-easternmost province of its empire; but for ten years, it made little effort to bring the unruly Texans to heel. Mexico's greatest fear was not that Texas should consider itself independent, but that it would be annexed by the United States. There was a good deal of popular support for annexation—most Texan settlers were Americans from the southern states, who chafed under Mexican anti-slavery laws. The southern states themselves were eager to add another slave state to the Union, while the northern states were bitterly opposed to any action that would make the pro-slavery factions in Congress any stronger than they were already. War began to loom after President John Tyler of Virginia, a slave owner himself, re-opened formal negotiations for annexation in 1844. Ostensibly to prevent the Mexican army from interfering in the negotiations, he ordered a large number of American soldiers—Grant's regiment among them—to take up position in disputed Texan territories along the Rio Grande. Open war began two years later, in 1846, after Texas was formally admitted to the Union.

By sheer coincidence, Grant had just departed Missouri on furlough to visit his family in Ohio when his regiment was dispatched to Louisiana in preparation for the outbreak of hostilities. A messenger was sent to bring Grant word and escort him back to the regiment, but it never caught up with him. He only learned how matters stood when a friend and fellow officer wrote to him in Ohio, warning him not to open any letters he might receive from the army. As it happened, no letters from the army ever appeared, so Grant remained in Ohio until his furlough was over. Dutiful though Grant was, he was just as relieved to postpone his return. Like Abraham Lincoln, who destroyed his chances of being re-elected to the House of Representatives after giving a speech on the floor of Congress stating his opposition to the war with Mexico, Grant bitterly disapproved of American interference in Texas. He later decried the Mexican-American War as "one of the most unjust ever waged by a stronger against a weaker nation." He believed that the American government was making the fatal mistake of mimicking its European forebears by waging a war, not for any morally justifiable cause, but simply to acquire more land. Furthermore, because the annexation of Texas so strengthened the position of the slave states, Grant would come to regard the conflict with Mexico as the strongest precipitating factor of the Civil War, which began only 12 years after its conclusion.

Grant's furlough was well-timed for another reason. While in Ohio, he had experienced a revelation regarding his feelings towards Julia Dent. Grant later wrote that, "if the 4th Infantry had remained at Jefferson Barracks, it is possible, even probable, that life might have continued for some years without my finding out that there was anything serious the matter with me." Perhaps the knowledge that war, with all its attendant hazards, lay in his immediate future had clarified his priorities. As soon as Grant returned to Jefferson Barracks, he visited the officer in charge and asked that his furlough be extended by a few days so that he could visit the Dents and speak with Julia. The officer agreed that he might as well do so, since it would make little difference whether Grant reached Louisiana a few days later than expected. This time, when speaking with Julia, Grant did not rely on symbolic gestures. He told her plainly that life without her would be "insupportable", and that he wished to marry her. Julia told him that she would like very much to be engaged, but she was not yet ready to be married. Grant gave her his ring, and Julia gave him a lock of her hair. Their engagement was to last for four years, until after Grant's regiment returned from Louisiana in July of 1848.

Grant's involvement in the Mexican-American War is interesting to biographers chiefly because it was a rehearsal, in many ways, for the later war that would make him famous. Most of the officers were West Point graduates like Grant, and many of them would go on to fight in the Civil War—some for the north, some for the south. The Mexican-American War also provided Grant with a role model whose example he would later strive to emulate—61-year old Zachary Taylor, who would be elected president after the war, though he would die after only five months in office. Grant thought highly of Taylor's command style.

Like Grant, Taylor eschewed the formalities and trappings of high military rank. He usually wore denim trousers, a duster, and a wide-brimmed hat, rather than an officer's uniform. Taylor preferred to rely on his own first-hand impressions, rather than reports from his subordinates, so he made daily tours of his camps, coming to know all of his officers and many of the enlisted men by name. Taylor also shared some of Grant's feelings about the dubious morality of the conflict he was embroiled in. He took a common sense approach to military discipline. He praised Grant on one occasion for being willing to climb into dirty water up to his knees in order to demonstrate to his men how to clear underwater obstacles from the river in preparation for a crossing. Grant's fellow officers, their uniforms dry and pristine, made fun of him from the safety of the river bank, but Taylor informed them that he wished he had many more officers like Grant, who weren't afraid to set a personal example for the men under their command. But when it came to more important matters, Taylor did not fail to make his expectations clear. Plunder, pillage, and rape, the traditional collateral damage that follows in the wake of a hostile army, were strictly forbidden under Taylor's command. Before the army set out for the Rio Grande, Taylor issued a written order declaring that the troops were "to observe, with the most scrupulous regard, the rights of all persons who may be found in the peaceful pursuit of their respective avocations. No person, under any pretense whatsoever, will interfere in any manner with the civil rights or religious privileges of the people, but will pay the utmost respect to both." Grant, impressed by the order, kept a copy of it with his things. Grant later wrote that Taylor "looked upon the enemy as the aggrieved party and was not willing to injure them further than his instructions from Washington demanded."

Grant corresponded with Julia regularly while his regiment was at war, though he, being a soldier longing for home comforts, wrote more frequently than Julia wrote to him. He was ill at ease with their engagement being kept secret, and in 1845 inquired whether she had yet told her mother about it. Soon he was writing to ask her whether it was not time for them to begin seriously planning for the wedding. Grant requested special leave to travel back to Missouri and formally request permission from Colonel and Mrs. Dent to marry their daughter. Julia's mother and brothers and sisters were overjoyed at the prospect, but Colonel Dent was hesitant; the life of an army officer's wife was difficult, since her husband would never live in any one place for very long, and the pay was not sufficient, in his eyes, to support a family. Julia's determination overcame her father's objection, however, and Grant later wrote to assure her that he meant to resign from the army as soon as it was possible to do so, and that even though the war had made his appointment as an instructor at West Point impossible to pursue, he had received an offer to teach mathematics at a well-regarded school in Ohio, where the pay would be equal or greater to the pay he received as a second lieutenant.

The Mexican-American War saw a greater percentage of American casualties than any other war fought in American history, including the Vietnam War. This was due largely to the fact no American army had ever mounted an assault in enemy territory before, and the logistics were as daunting as the officers were poorly prepared. There was no shortage of volunteers, especially from the southern states, but as one Grant biographer writes, the southerners were "so accustomed to slaves that they were unable to cut their own wood or draw their own water."

A letter written by George Meade, then Taylor's chief army engineer, later the Union general who defeated Robert E. Lee at Gettysburg, described the "loud complaints" that were being made by both the Texan and American volunteers, because Taylor was advancing too slowly for their tastes. According to Meade, the volunteers balked at the amount of work Taylor demanded of them, saying "it is all nonsense to take such a quantity of supplies, [and that] they never carried wagons and such things. True enough, but what was the result? Why, when [the Texans] met the enemy, an hour's fight *exhausted* all their *ammunition*, and they had to retire, and when they retired, they abandoned their sick and wounded on the field. And if a man was taken sick on a march he was left, to join them if he could get well, if not, to die alone in the midst of the prairie; and after they took a place, they had to abandon it in a few days, because they had no means of holding it. This is not our plan. When we advance it is for some object, and we shall have the means of holding every advantage we gain, of taking care of our people en route, and being able to fight several battles before our ammunition gives out. But to do this, preparations must be made, and preparations require time in every country, but most particularly in this."

Taylor too was concerned with supply and logistics. Under his command, Grant was appointed the quartermaster of his regiment. Grant possessed a few skills that were rare in the American army—chiefly his mathematical abilities, which were suited to keeping track of large numbers of men, munitions, and other supplies. His legendary skills on horseback were also taken into account, as the army had recently purchased almost two thousand pack mules, and it was thought Grant could manage them better than a less skilled rider. (This proved an overly optimistic hope.) Grant had no desire to be a quartermaster, however; such a position would keep him far from the front lines, and he bitterly resented being removed from "sharing in the dangers and honors of service with my company at the front." His commanding officer, however, informed him that he had been made quartermaster because of "his observed ability, skill, and persistency in the line of duty", going on to add that "Lieutenant Grant can best serve his country in present emergencies under this assignment." Little though Grant liked it, the experience he gained serving as quartermaster would prove invaluable to him during the Civil War. Union soldiers under Grant's command never lacked for food or ammunition, making them luckier than most of the soldiers who fought in that war.

By the time of the critical Mexican defeat during the Battle of Monterrey in September of 1846, Grant was back with his regiment, serving as an adjutant. Both sides suffered heavy casualties, and in the aftermath, Zachary Taylor negotiated a two-month ceasefire with Mexican general

Pedro de Ampudia. In returning for the surrender of Black Fort, Ampudia's army would be permitted to retreat without surrendering their arms or colors. Taylor was heavily criticized for offering Ampudia such liberal terms, and President Polk in particular claimed that Taylor had exceeded his authority by offering the ceasefire—his feeling was that Taylor should have taken advantage of his victory by crushing what remained of Ampudia's forces. But Grant and Meade, who were watching from the front lines, felt differently. There was "no military necessity that induced General Taylor to grant such liberal terms, but a higher and nobler motive," Meade wrote. "First, to grant an opportunity to the two governments to negotiate for peace. Second, to stop the unnecessary effusion of blood, not only of soldiers, but of women and children who were crowded in with the troops. Third, as a tribute to the gallantry of the Mexicans, who had defended their place as long as it was in their power." Twenty years later, when accepting General Lee's surrender at

Appomattox, Grant would offer the surrendering Confederates "virtually identical" terms, permitting the officers to keep their swords and the men to keep their personal possessions.

The chief lesson which the Mexican-American War taught Grant, as a young officer, was that professionalism was of paramount importance to an army's success. Professionalism did not reside, as some officers believed, in formalities and appearances and a strict separation between the common fighting men and the officers, but rather in issuing orders that were both sensible and clearly conveyed, in meticulous plotting and strategizing, maintaining supply lines, and keeping the respect of the fighting men, so that they would always know what was expected of them. Grant's post-mortem analysis of the war after the Mexican defeat reveals an awareness that the size of an army is not the only indicator of its ability to win great victories:

"At the battles of Palo Alto and Resaca de la Palma, General Taylor had a small army, but it was composed exclusively of regular troops, under the best of drill and discipline. Every officer, from the highest to the lowest, was educated for his profession, not at West Point necessarily, but in the camp, in garrison, and many of them in Indian wars. The rank and file were probably inferior to the volunteers that participated in the later battles of the war; but they were brave men, and drill and discipline brought out all there was in them... The volunteers who followed were of better material, but without drill or discipline at the start. They were associated with so many disciplined men and professionally educated officers, that when they went into engagements it was with a confidence they would not have felt otherwise. They became soldiers themselves almost at once."

There was another, potentially equally valuable kind of experience gained by Grant during the war. Just as the war itself was the proving ground for virtually all the West Point men who were still serving as active military at the time, the veterans of the Mexican-American War formed the backbone of the officer class that would lead both the Union and Confederate armies in just over a decade's time. Grant served with Henry W. Halleck, George B. McClellan, Joseph Hooker, George Henry Thomas, William Tecumseh Sherman, and Don Carlos Buell, all of whom would serve with him or under him as Union officers during the Civil War. On the Confederate side, Grant's fellow Mexican-American War veterans included Stonewall Jackson, D.H. Hill, Braxton Bragg, Joseph E. Johnston, Robert E. Lee, P.G.T. Beauregard, Simon Bolivar Buckner, and his close friend James Longstreet. Grant would later grow conscious that his personal knowledge of many of the same men "who afterwards became generals on one side or the other in the rebellion...holding high commands" was of "immense service" to him.

"I do not pretend that all movements, or even many of them, were made with special reference to the characteristics of the commander against whom they were directed," Grant later wrote. "But my appreciation of my enemies was certainly affected by this knowledge. The natural disposition of most people is to clothe a commander of a large army with superhuman abilities. A large part of the National [Union] army, for instance, and most of the press of the country, clothed General Lee with such abilities. But I had known him personally, and knew that he was mortal; and it was just as well that I felt this."

# Chapter Two: Brother Against Brother

## Resignation from the army

"Since my last letter," Grant wrote to Julia Dent, in September of 1847, "four of the hardest fought battles that the world ever witnessed have taken place, and the most astonishing victories have crowned the American arms. But dearly have they paid for it. The loss of officers and men killed and wounded is frightful...out of all the [twenty-one] officers that left Jefferson Barracks with the 4th Infantry, only three besides myself now remain with us." Now that American victory had been achieved and fighting had come to an end, Grant was part of the occupying force left behind in Mexico to serve in the place of the absent Mexican government. Grant had come to love Mexico and think highly of its people and its natural beauties; all the same, he had a fiancée waiting at home, and he missed Julia desperately. He wrote to her once a month, which was as often as the mail wagons made their rounds. They had been engaged for four years, and during all that time they had seen each other only once, when Grant had obtained special leave to visit the Dents and ask for their permission to marry Julia.

Finally, in the summer of 1848, American forces began to withdraw from Mexico. Grant was reunited with Julia in July of that year, and the wedding date was set for late August. Though at one time he had had to reassure Julia's father that he did not intend to remain in the army after the war, but would find a more stable and lucrative position as a mathematics professor at West Point or some other school, he had by now put aside his thoughts of resigning. Grant had been promoted to first lieutenant, and in addition to a significant increase in pay, his elevated position came with "rations for his family and fodder for his horses", which meant he would be well able to provide for a family. When the wedding took place on August 22, 1848, the groom's party included James Longstreet as best man and Cadmus Wilcox and Bernard Pratte as ushers. All three men would go on to serve as high-ranking Confederate officers. None of Grant's own family attended the wedding, due to the fact that his father Jesse, an ardent abolitionist, strongly disapproved of his son's marriage to the daughter of a prominent slave owner.

Having returned from the war on the southern border of the United States, Grant was assigned to the defense of the northern border shortly after his marriage. He was posted to Michigan, first to Sackets Harbor, then to Detroit, where he and Julia set up housekeeping and celebrated the birth of their first child, Frederick Dent Grant, in the spring of 1850. In 1852, however, after the start of the California gold rush, Grant's regiment was dispatched to California to help keep the peace. Julia was unable to accompany him, though the wives and families of the other officers were being provided for, because she was eight months pregnant with their second child. It was decided that she would stay with Grant's family, then with her own, and that Grant would send for her as soon as it was safe to do so. It proved a bitter parting, more so for Grant than for Julia. A lifelong loner, he had come to understand what it meant to share his life with a woman he loved and depended upon. Being thrust back into a bachelor lifestyle suited him very poorly.

It was just as well that Julia had remained behind however, as the journey to California by way of Panama was a disaster that resulted in the loss of many lives, mostly to cholera. Grant helped to nurse the sick himself, setting an example of cool-headedness for the orderlies who had balked at tending the cholera sufferers for fear of becoming infected themselves. "The horrors are beyond description," he wrote in a letter to Julia along the way. "Every child of Fred's age or younger, and there were twenty of them, either died on the crossing or shortly thereafter." Friends of Grant's would recall later that he dwelt with more regret upon the memory of the Panama crossing than on any of the battles he had fought, in any war. When Grant became president, he proposed that a canal be built in Panama to link the Atlantic and Pacific oceans, a measure he felt would have prevented much of the suffering he witnessed in 1852.

Once Grant and the 4th Infantry—what remained of it—arrived in San Francisco, he quickly succumbed to the "gold fever" that ran as rampant through the city as any disease. In northern California in the 1850s, one didn't need to be a gold prospector in order to strike it rich. There was so much wealth in the area, and so comparatively few settlers, that anyone with a valuable skill could find lucrative ventures suited to their abilities. Grant's fellow officers were making large piles of cash in their off-duty hours by working as lawyers, or speculating in land. Grant himself wrote to Julia that if he resigned from the army he could probably make enough money in a year to keep them comfortable for the rest of their lives—but that he was not seriously considering it, because "what I have is a certainty, and what I might expect to do might prove a dream." Nonetheless, he regarded men like Julia's two brothers, who had found considerable wealth in California by owning and operating a hotel and a ferry service, with considerable envy. He had only been in San Francisco for four months, however, when he was transferred north to Fort Vancouver—and there, financial disaster struck. Grant embarked on a series of business deals with partners who proved either swindlers, or incompetents. A farming venture was destroyed by flooding. Every time Grant made a profit, it was quickly swept away. "Neither Grant nor myself had the slightest suggestion of business talent," was the mournful assessment of one of his ill-chosen partners. "He was the perfect soul of honor and truth, and believed everyone as artless as he was himself."

In despair over his financial losses and his separation from his family—he missed Julia more than ever, and his second son, Ulysses, was three months old before any of Julia's letters managed to reach California—Grant began drinking. His reputation as a drunkard, which followed him through his career in the Union army, was only partially deserved. Grant seems to have suffered from a genetic condition called alcohol intolerance, or allergy to alcohol. In the words of one biographer, "a couple of swallows [of liquor] slurred his speech, and a drink or two made him drunk." His actual alcohol consumption was far more moderate than that of most of his fellow officers. "He would perhaps go on two or three sprees a year," one of his friends recalled, "but was always open to reason, and when spoken to on the subject would own up and promise to stop drinking, which he did." It is possible that Grant's heightened sensitivity to alcohol actually prevented him from developing a more severe drinking problem, since he was simply incapable of imbibing enough liquor to form a physical dependency that would have made abstention extremely difficult or impossible.

In August of 1853, Grant was promoted to the rank of captain, which brought with it a pay increase and the position of company commander. He was notified of the promotion by none other than Secretary of War Jefferson Davis, future president of the Confederacy, who ordered him to "proceed, without delay, to join your company (F) at Fort Humboldt, California." It was considered a plum posting compared to Fort Vancouver, but there were no accommodations for officer's families, and Grant's misery over the enforced separation from

Julia was intensified by the fact that not a single letter from her had yet reached him, and the mail runs were even more infrequent at Fort Humboldt than they had been at his previous posting. Furthermore, his promotion from lieutenant and quartermaster to captain had left him with little to do, and for a man of Grant's temperament—he depended on exertion and activity in order to keep his spirits up—the idleness was ruinous. His drinking "sprees" became more frequent.

Suddenly one day in 1854, Grant submitted the following letter to his commanding officer:

"I very respectfully tender my resignation of my commission as an officer of the Army, and request that it may take effect from the 31st of July next. Very respectfully, Yr. Obt. Svt., U.S. Grant, Captain 4th Inf.

There is no official, incontrovertible explanation on record for Grant's resignation, or the abruptness of it, but those who knew him during the years of his California postings had their own explanation to offer. Rufus Ingalls, who had been friends with Grant since their West Point days, claimed that his resignation had come about in the manner described below:

"Grant, finding himself in dreary surroundings, without his family, and with but little to occupy his attention, fell into dissipated habits, and was found one day, too much under the influence of liquor to properly perform his duties. For this offense Colonel Buchanan demanded that he should resign, or stand trial. Grant's friends at the time urged him to stand trial, and were confident of his acquittal; but, actuated by a noble spirit, he said he would not for all the world have his wife know that he had been tried on such a charge. He therefore resigned his commission, and return to civil life."

It was unlike Grant to do anything abruptly, without considering all the ramifications first, and though he had repeatedly flirted with the idea of resigning from the army in his letters to Julia, he had always refrained from any absolute determination in that direction. The specter of potential poverty was too dire to face. Grant would later say that he had resigned because he could not support his family on his salary while they were living so far away from him, but he also admitted that "the vice of intemperance had not a little to do with my decision to resign." Colonel Buchanan, during the Civil War, was pressed to disclose the reason for Grant's leaving the army, and while he would not give details, he did admit that he had given Grant a choice between resigning and standing trial.

## Hardscrabble

Grant had to rely on the generosity of friends in order to make his way back to the east coast, where he arrived in New York on June 25, 1854. Once there, he did not immediately set out for Ohio. It seems as though he was afraid that news of his disgraceful departure from the army had reached Julia, and that he was afraid she would not want him to return home. Before leaving California he had written her a brief note telling her of his return and asking her to direct future letters to New York, but when he found no letter waiting for him in that city, he felt that he had to remain where he was until he heard from her. (Julia Grant later wrote in her memoirs that her husband told her, "You know I had to wait in New York until I heard from you.") While he was waiting, he ran out of money, and again had to apply to friends to help him settle his bills. Eventually, a letter from Julia did reach him, and it assured Grant that she and his two children, including the two-year old son he had never met, were eagerly anticipating his homecoming. With money borrowed from his father, Grant set out for Ohio to be reunited with them.

In his memoirs, Grant wrote that,

"In the late summer of 1854 I rejoined my family, to find a son I had never seen. I was now to commence, at the age of thirty-two, a new struggle for our support. My wife had a farm near St. Louis, to which we went, but I had no means to stock it. A house had to be built also. I worked very hard, never losing a day because of bad weather, and accomplished the object in a moderate way. If nothing else could be done I would load a cord of wood on a wagon and take it to the city for sale. I managed to keep along fairly well until 1858, when I was attacked by fever and ague. It lasted over a year, and, while it did not keep me in the house, it did interfere greatly with the amount of work I was able to perform. In

1858 I sold out my stock, crops, and farming utensils at auction and gave up farming."

Grant's circumstances were dire and luck seemed to turn against him at every venture, but there was no blaming alcohol this time—he no longer drank at all. Old army friends from Jefferson Barracks who ran into Grant noted that he would accompany them into the bar, but wouldn't touch a drop while there. Yet nothing improved, despite his sobriety. After suffering heavy losses at Hardscrabble (the wry name which he and Julia had bestowed upon their 60-acre farm), Julia's parents decided to vacate their summer home, White Haven, and rent it to Grant, along with two servants and one slave, a man in his mid-thirties named William Jones. After Grant failed to to farm White Haven successfully, Colonel Dent arranged for him to take up employment at a real estate agency owned by the Colonel's nephew. But Grant evidenced no greater talent for business in St. Louis than he had as a prospector in California, and though the real estate market was booming, Boggs & Grant seemed to be the only agency in town that was failing to turn a profit.

By the summer of 1859, the firm was out of business, and Grant was forced to look for work once more. By this point, William Jones had become Grant's property, most likely a gift from Colonel Dent, since Grant had never owned a slave before in his life and did not have the money to purchase one even if he so desired. For a time, Grant considered renting Jones out as a laborer, a common way of using slaves to generate income, but in the end he did something quite different: he had manumission papers drawn up, setting Jones free. For a man of Grant's time and circumstances, this was an extraordinary act. Had he sold William Jones at auction, he could have made at least a thousand dollars on the sale, the equivalent of a year's salary at his old army rank of captain. It is worth noting that when Grant filed manumission papers for Jones on March 29, 1859, he was very nearly the poorest he had ever been in his life, and could undoubtedly have put a sum of a thousand dollars to good use. The fact that he chose to set Jones free rather than keep him or sell him is all the more remarkable in light of the fact that Grant, who abhorred politics and saw slavery as an essentially political question, had never thought of himself as being especially opposed to slavery. His father Jesse was a vehement abolitionist, and perhaps this had something to do with forming Grant's seemingly unexamined feelings on the subject. But it is equally likely that, never having owned a slave or spent much time around those who did, his own well-established sense of honor and justice made it impossible for him to retain a human being as his personal property.

Grant's fortunes did not begin to turn until Julia persuaded him to go visit his father and ask for a job in his tannery business. Since boyhood, Grant had been determined never to work for his father's company, but by now he was too desperate for such pride. Jesse Grant made him a clerk in his offices at Galena, Illinois, where he would be working alongside his two younger brothers, Simpson and Orvil. The salary was less than half of what he had made at previous jobs, but there was security in it at least. At long last, at the age of 38, he began to feel that he could live the happy, modest life with his wife and children he had always wanted. "Had peace prevailed," notes one biographer, "he would have lived out his days as a slightly rumpled shopkeeper in the upper Mississippi valley, indistinguishable from his friends and neighbors." But in 1860, shortly after the inauguration of Abraham Lincoln as president, southern states began seceding from the Union one by one. By April 12, 1861, Confederate soldiers had fired on Fort Sumter, and the Civil War had begun.

**"The quiet man"**

Lincoln's initial call for 75,000 volunteers to meet the Confederate armies being raised in the south was met with tremendous enthusiasm and willingness on the part of the average northerner. Volunteers for the state regiments flooded the recruiting offices. Grant, a professional soldier who had served in the army for eleven years, knew that his skills could be of use. Each state was required to supply a certain number of volunteer regiments according to its size; Illinois was asked to provide six, and there was no difficulty finding enough enlisted men. The officers, too, were plentiful, but placing them in the army was by no means as simple as signing up at a recruiter's office. As the only man in Galena, Illinois, who had any military experience, Grant was highly sought after in the spring and summer of 1860 as the one man who knew how to organize troop mobilization on a large scale. But he had difficulty obtaining an officer's commission. Commissions were granted at the recommendation of high-ranking politicians, and Grant found himself surrounded by men who were willing to jockey for position and trade favors in order to obtain a suitably high command. Grant found this sort of "wire-pulling", as he referred to it, highly distasteful. As a West Point man and a distinguished veteran of the Mexican-American War, he "declined to receive endorsement for permission to fight for [his] country". Instead, he made his availability known to a number of people—including his old West Point associates—and waited to be told what he should do.

Grant had difficulty obtaining a commission partly for the same reason he found it so impossible to succeed at any commercial enterprise: his notions of honor were too rarefied for the grubby business of trading favors. Apart from this, some of his old army contacts were snubbing him because of the manner of his resignation from the army seven years earlier. McClellan, whose staff Grant attempted to join, still thought of Grant as a man with a drinking problem, though he had rarely touched alcohol since being reunited with his family, and certainly never went out on "sprees" any more. Others who did not know about the drinking problem that plagued him in California simply found the abruptness of his resignation suspicious. There were, at least in 1860, too many Union officers with impeccable records to choose from, most of whom had politicians in their corner.

Grant had suffered years of poverty, only to achieve stability after going to work for his father's tannery business. Now, having resigned his position in his father's company, and unable to obtain a commission, he was rapidly returning to the same straitened circumstances as before. Eager to be of service to his country in any way possible, Grant began to contemplate going into business as a baker to supply the army's commissary—he had established a profitable bread-baking business while he was stationed in Mexico after the war. Before he had to resort to such measures, however, Illinois governor Richard Yates came to Grant's rescue. Grant's name had been mentioned to Yates by Illinois Congressman Elihu Washburne, a Springfield politician and close friend of Abraham Lincoln's. Unlike other politicians who had approached Grant, Washburne had not attempted to bargain with Grant over his endorsement, but had simply informed Grant that his services were needed, and he must remain in the area until something could be arranged for him. This straightforward approach succeeded with Grant where other forms of persuasion had not. After working for a time in the state adjutant general's office, sorting out "the chaos of [statewide] mobilization", Grant served as a mustering officer and aide to the governor. His duty as a mustering officer entailed swearing in the regiments from the various congressional districts, thereby making them official regiments of the Union army. The men of one regiment, the 21st Illinois, took a particular liking to Grant. A few weeks after Grant visited them, the 21st ousted their own elected colonel and demanded a new commanding officer—"preferably Captain Grant", they said. Governor Yates accordingly sent Grant a telegram offering him the command of the regiment, and it was with a deep sense of relief that Grant took up his duties.

The men of the 21st Illinois regiment soon dubbed their new commanding colonel "the quiet man". Like Zachary Taylor, whose professional yet easygoing manner with his officers and men had made such an impression on Grant during his last war, Grant emphasized professionalism and common sense to the men serving under him. The regiment was in dire need of both qualities. Grant held his officers and non-commissioned officers alike to a higher standard than the enlisted men. To his way of thinking, there was, and ought to be, a distinction between West Point-trained men who had spent four years studying warfare in classrooms at the government's expense, and men who until recently had been farmers or laborers. The duty of the commissioned officers was to clearly explain to the non-commissioned officers their responsibilities in training and drilling the men. The duty of the enlisted men was to learn their drills and absorb from their officers the discipline that would help keep them alive on the battlefield.

The 21st had rebelled against their previous commander because he did not understand them, and they did not respect him. What Zachary Taylor had understood, and what Grant had learned during his seven years of civilian life, was that the rigid military discipline that West

Pointers and career soldiers took for granted seemed utterly arbitrary and meaningless to men who had only just put down their plows and picked up their rifles in defense of their country. As such, Grant relaxed certain regulations while emphasizing others. Possibly remembering the habits of life in Mexico, Grant made a point of not scheduling drills between noon and 5 pm, when the summer sun was blazing at its hottest. His men, officers and enlisted alike, were free to come and go from the camp whenever they liked, so long as they showed up promptly for drills and roll call. "In extending this privilege to the men of this command," Grant wrote in his orders, "the Colonel Commanding hopes that this leniency will not be so abused as to make it necessary to restrict it. All men when out of Camp should reflect that they are Gentlemen—in camp, soldiers; and the Commanding Officer hopes that all of his command will sustain these two characters with fidelity." This order, which reflected Grant's genuine respect for the ordinary men in his regiment, a respect not always found in officers of his rank, had a "wonderful" effect on discipline. Men who were unused to military hierarchy suddenly showed themselves willing to submit to it, because the rules now made sense to them.

Grant won even more respect from the enlisted men of the 21st after he left camp for a few days in order to provide himself with a uniform and other supplies, only to discover upon his return that the camp had fallen to pieces in his absence. Officers had begun taking a casual approach to turning up for drills, and several men posted on guard duty had deserted their posts and been confined to the barracks. During wartime, desertion of a guard post was punishable by death. But Grant understood that men who were new to military life probably had no concept of how serious their offense had been. Rather than subjecting them to a court martial and a firing squad, Grant simply explained to them how matters stood, and warned them that a second offense would be met with the punishments prescribed by the Articles of War. The officers who had neglected to drill their men were met with more serious consequences: they were no longer permitted to leave the camp in the evenings without his explicit permission, though the enlisted men were under no such restriction.

Grant's sense of justice resonated strongly with the men in his command. It was not lost on them that when Grant had to administer disciplinary action, he did so "in a quiet way, and in a spirit that did not enrage the one punished." In other words, Grant managed to enforce discipline without resorting to humiliation. The regiment's chaplain, James Crane, later wrote that Grant "would correct every infraction on the spot, but in as cool and unruffled a manner as you would give directions to your gardener before breakfast." Grant, whose modesty ran so deep that it had nearly prevented him from gaining a commission, had no need to break his men down in order to build up his own ego.

As soon as the 21st had been officially mustered into the Union army, Grant was ordered to move them to the Mississippi River, near the border with Missouri. Along with Delaware, Maryland, and Kentucky, Missouri was one of the four "border states"—slave states that chose not to secede. The fate of the war essentially depended on the border states remaining loyal to the Union, but in Missouri particularly there was strong support for the Confederacy and a popular secessionist movement. Grant's regiment was part of a larger movement to reinforce Union troops in that state, to prevent secessionists from undermining Union loyalists there. Grant annoyed Washington by marching his regiment the 116 miles from Springfield to his new posting in Quincy, Illinois, rather than traveling by rail. Grant's reasoning was simple: "This is an infantry regiment. The men are going to do a lot of marching before the war is over and I prefer to train them in friendly country, not in the enemy's." The 21st Illinois regiment set out from home on July 3, 1851.

Grant was unexpectedly promoted to brigadier general while his regiment was in northern Missouri, policing a relatively peaceful yet ostensibly hostile territory. He only learned of the promotion because his regimental chaplain happened to read about it in a newspaper. Congressman Washburne, Grant correctly guessed, had mentioned Grant's name to Lincoln after the president received authorization from Congress to create 34 new brigadier generals, and Lincoln had added Grant's name to the roster on Washburne's recommendation. This made Grant 35th in the chain of command of the Union army, then headed by General Winfield Scott.

The principle business of the Union army in the west was to gain control of the Mississippi River. Via the Mississippi, Missouri, Illinois, Kentucky, and Tennessee were all potential staging points for Confederate assaults, should the Union fail to seize control of it. Major General John C. Frémont intended for the army of the west to "capture Memphis, [and] lop off Vicksburg and New Orleans" after which, it was thought, "the Confederacy would wither." Against advice, he chose Grant as the field commander to lead the combined Union offensive. Frémont had been advised of Grant's reputation as a heavy drinker, but after meeting him in person, Frémont was convinced that Grant was the man for the job. "I believe him to be a man of great activity and promptness in obeying orders without question or hesitation," Frémont later explained. "For that reason I gave General Grant this important command at this critical period. I did not consider him then a great general, for the qualities that led him to success had not had the opportunity for their development. I selected him for qualities I could not then find combined in any other officer, for General Grant was a man of unassuming character, not given to self-elation, of dogged persistence, and iron will."

# Chapter Three: "Unconditional Surrender" Grant

## Paducah

As of August 30, 1861, Grant was in command, not merely of the 21st Illinois regiment, but of "all Union forces in southeastern Missouri and southern Illinois". His orders were to "occupy Columbus in Kentucky as soon as possible...to establish a base for operations against Memphis and Nashville." Before Grant set out to fulfill these orders, Frémont gave him a final piece of advice: now that he was a general, he should really exchange the shabby civilian clothing he wore for a proper uniform. Grant, possibly for the first time in his military career, was daunted by the enormity of the responsibility that had been entrusted to him. "You should be cheerful and try to encourage," he wrote in a letter to his wife. "I have a task before me of no trifling moment and want all the encouragement possible. The safety of the country, to some extent, and my reputation and that of our children, greatly depends upon my acts."

Grant intended to seize Columbus, Kentucky, from the staging ground of Cairo, Illinois, which sits at the confluence of the Ohio and Mississippi rivers. But no sooner had he arrived in Cairo than he discovered that the Confederate army had taken Columbus already. Kentucky, as a border state, was technically neutral, but pro-secession factions had invited the Confederates to march to the defense of Columbus when they realized that Union soldiers were on the move. At stake was control of the Mobile & Ohio Railroad, which connected what was then the western American frontier to the Gulf Coast. Upon learning that the Confederate army had beaten him to Columbus, Grant, undaunted, informed Frémont that unless he received orders to the contrary, he intended to march around Columbus and seize the town of Paducah.

Control of Paducah would give the Union forces access to the Ohio and Tennessee rivers, providing an alternative waterway to Mississippi that led into the heart of the Confederacy.

Grant managed to seize Paducah without firing a single shot, and without triggering any of the potentially dire political consequences that might have arisen from the presence of the Union army in a technically neutral state. The people of Paducah were understandably dismayed and frightened when they saw the Union army marching in—they had been expecting the Confederates to arrive from Columbus later that day. Grant had telegrammed the state legislature before making his advance to notify them that Kentucky had already been invaded, and its neutrality violated, by the Confederates, with the implication that he had come to expel the invaders and liberate the state. As Kentucky was the birthplace of Abraham Lincoln, it was especially important that military discipline be maintained, the rights of citizens be respected, and as little blood as possible be shed by Union soldiers. Accordingly, Grant did not remain in Paducah long, but seized control of the railroad, seized supplies that had been intended for Leonidas Polk's Confederate forces, and returned to his former position at Cairo. Before leaving Paducah, Grant issued a proclamation, in the hopes of soothing any ruffled feathers his occupation was leaving behind:

"To the Citizens of Paducah!

"I have come among you, not as an enemy, but as your friend and fellow-citizen, not to injure or annoy you, but to respect the rights, and to defend and enforce the rights of all loyal citizens. An enemy, in rebellion against our common Government, has taken possession of, and planted its guns upon the soil of Kentucky and fired upon our flag. Hickman and Columbus are in his hands. He is moving upon your city. I am here to defend you against this enemy and to assert and maintain the authority and sovereignty of your Government and mine. I have nothing to do with opinions. I shall deal only with armed rebellion and its aiders and abettors. You can pursue your usual avocations without fear or hindrance. The strong arm of the Government is here to protect its friends, and to punish only its enemies. Whenever it is manifest that you are able to defend yourselves, to maintain the authority of your government and protect the rights of all its loyal citizens, I shall withdraw the forces under my command from your city."

Grant issued orders along the same lines to the men he was leaving behind, charging them to "take special care and precaution that no harm is done to inoffensive citizens...[S]oldiers shall not enter any private dwelling nor make any private searches unless by [Grant's subordinate, General

Eleazar Paine's] orders. Exercise the strictest discipline against any soldier who shall insult citizens, or engage in plundering private property." In issuing such orders, Grant was setting important precedents for the conduct of the Union army when it came into territory regarded as potentially hostile.

After Grant left Paducah, Frémont placed General Charles Ferguson Smith in charge of the city and ordered Grant to proceed down the Mississippi. He himself was preparing to drive the Confederates out of the Kentucky city of Lexington—a last ditch effort to restore his credibility in the eyes of President Lincoln, who was furious with Frémont after he declared martial law in Missouri and began executing Confederate sympathizers and freeing their slaves in contravention of the law. (The Emancipation Proclamation, declaring that all slaves in Confederate hands were free under federal law, had not yet been issued.) Grant, along with Smith, wanted to take Columbus now that the Confederate position in Kentucky had been weakened. Frémont neither expressly forbade nor expressly authorized the move, but soon, his opinion was irrelevant; though he succeeded in driving Confederate troops from Lexington he failed to crush them, and the main strength of the army slipped away to regroup. Lincoln withdrew Frémont's command and put Grant's old friend Henry W. Halleck in his place.

## Belmont

The day before Frémont was relieved of his command, he gave two final sets of orders to Grant: to "make demonstrations with your troops" in the vicinity of Columbus, so as to threaten and antagonize Leonidas Polk, and to find the Confederate cavalry led by General M. Jeff Thompson, which was harassing Union troops along the banks of the St. Francis River. Frémont ordered Grant to "drive him back to Arkansas." Grant, as would prove to be his tendency throughout the war, believed that every engagement with the enemy should be pursued as an opportunity to destroy the enemy entirely. Frémont had ordered him to chase Thompson back south, but Grant intended to destroy Thompson's Belmont, Missouri headquarters, while also finishing Polk's forces in Columbus, with the help of Charles Ferguson Smith, who was still holding Paducah. Grant informed Smith that he was "fitting out an expedition to menace Belmont and will take all the force proper to spare from here. If you can make a demonstration toward Columbus at the same time with a portion of your command, it would probably keep the enemy from throwing over the river much more force than they now have there, and might enable me to drive those they have there out of Missouri." Geographically, Belmont was positioned just across the Mississippi River from Columbus—seizing both cities at once would strike a major blow against Confederate power in the west.

Technically speaking, Grant was under orders not to engage Polk's forces in Columbus, and his ambitions for seizing Belmont required that he play fast and loose with military regulations. But Grant believed that the Union was in danger of losing the opportunity to make the advance down the Mississippi unless the Confederates were routed there soon. He was also aware that his soldiers were spoiling for a fight; the everyday boredom and drudgery and drills that made up a soldier's life in camps was hard for the volunteer fighters to weather. Yet it was only after Frémont was relieved of his command that Grant could strike without making himself guilty of violating a direct order from a superior. Grant's attitude was that, even if he was overreaching, all would be forgiven should he be victorious. But unbeknownst to him, Leonidas Polk had received advance warning that Grant was heading towards Belmont, and when Grant's forces made their approach they were met with heavy musket fire. A morning and afternoon of fighting in cornfields and thick forest resulted in the Confederate encampment being successfully overrun. But Grant's forces, though they had been rigorously drilled for battle, were less prepared for victory than they were in defeat. Any armed regiment can follow an order to retreat, but it took greater discipline to remain organized after the enemy appeared to be vanquished. Overjoyed Union soldiers dropped their weapons and began looting the Confederate camp. As a result, a large number of Confederate soldiers were able to escape and hide in the underbrush. If any Union soldiers had gone looking for them, the rebel soldiers would have had no choice but to surrender. Instead, they were able to creep back across the river, where Leonidas Polk was watching Grant's men fall into disarray.

Grant had been counting on the two gunships that had carried his men upriver to shield his flank. During the fighting however, they had been forced to retreat after drawing fire from Confederate artillery. Polk brought fight regiments of reinforcements across the river, and while the Union soldiers were still running roughshod over the remains of the Confederate camp, he opened fire. Grant, taken by surprise, attempted to call his soldiers to order once again, but it took so long to catch their attention that they had no option except to retreat. "We were demoralized," reported one officer present at the scene. "Officers would call to their men to fall in but the men would pay no attention. Every man was trying to save himself, some would throw down their arms and part of a regiment would take one route and the other part start another way." When Grant's men discovered a solid line of Confederate artillery waiting to cut off their retreat, they immediately concluded that surrender was their only option. But Grant informed them that that "we cut our way in and we can cut our way out." Colonel John Logan, commander of the 31st Illinois regiment, rode at the head of the column which broke the Confederate line, and Grant's men followed him to safety.

Belmont was only one in a series of embarrassing defeats that plagued the Union army in the second year of the Civil War. Each battle seemed to follow a set pattern: the Union army would appear in force, causing the Confederates to scatter, only to rally again and return to drive the Union forces from the field. Grant's casualties and losses were approximately equal to Polk's, but the loss of some 19% of his men was no trifling matter. He now had to own up to his defeat, but not until he was writing his personal memoirs, long after the war was over, did Grant admit that he had carried out the Belmont attack against orders. Frémont's removal from command created enough confusion to provide him with cover. Grant's own telegram to Union headquarters in St. Louis was obfuscatory: "We met the rebels about nine o'clock this morning two and a half miles from Belmont, drove them step by step into their camp and across the river. We burned their tents and started on our return with all their artillery... The rebels recrossed the river and followed in our rear to place of embarkation. Loss heavy on both sides." Even reading between the lines, it was difficult to tell whether such a telegram told a story of a qualified victory or a messy defeat. Union newspapers, however, decided that it had been a victory—probably because they were hungry for one. A St. Louis newspaper reported that Grant was "present where the balls flew thickest, directing every movement as calmly as if on parade." Thanks to reports of this nature, Grant's star began to rise in earnest.

## "Unconditional Surrender" Grant

Part of the reason for Grant's steady rise through the ranks of command during the Civil War was that he and President Lincoln shared a remarkably similar outlook on warfare. Grant admired men like Halleck, who was nicknamed "Old Brains", because of his strategic brilliance and his ability to conduct warfare from the remove of his command tent. But Grant himself was always more at home on the battlefield, and that is where his talents were displayed to best advantage. He believed that battle was the chief object of a soldier's professional life. Grant never called for reinforcements, rarely caviled over orders received, and possessed a general reputation for achieving desired results with the men and resources at his disposal, rather than insisting that his orders were impossible to carry out unless he was given one thing or the other. Compared to Grant, other prominent Union generals, such as George McClellan, were so hesitant to engage the enemy that Lincoln came to feel they were overly cautious, frustratingly reluctant to take risks. He expressed this frustration, on January 27, 1862, in the form of the President's General War Order No. 1:

"Ordered that the 22nd. day of February 1862, be the day for a general movement of the Land and Naval forces of the United States against the insurgent forces.

That especially --

The Army at & about Fortress Monroe

The Army of the Potomac

The Army of Western Virginia

The Army near Munfordsville, Ky.

The Army and Flotilla at Cairo

And a Naval force in the Gulf of Mexico, be ready for a movement on that day.

That all other forces, both Land and Naval, with their respective commanders, obey existing orders, for the time, and be ready to obey additional orders when duly given.

That the Heads of Departments, and especially the Secretaries of War and of the Navy, with all their subordinates; and the General-in-Chief, with all other commanders and subordinates, of Land and Naval forces, will severally be held to their strict and full responsibilities, for the prompt execution of this order."

Lincoln did not follow this statement with a specific plan of engagement—he left that to his generals. He merely wished to make it known that he expected them to engage the Confederate armies more aggressively than they had in 1860 or 1861. The armies must move, and the war hastened to its conclusion, before the federal government was defeated by its own bankruptcy—the war was costing the United States around four million dollars a day.

Lincoln's call for more aggressive tactics suited Grant admirably. And it would not be long before Grant came to Lincoln's attention as the one general in his army who would, whatever his other failings, always choose to fight rather than hold back and make fruitless assessments.

Because the presidential war order specifically referenced "the Army and Flotilla at Cairo", Grant suddenly had tacit license to come up with his own battle plans and then put them to his superiors in the form of suggestions that were not easily ignored. The day after Lincoln's order was issued, Grant wired Halleck with his plans to advance the Union army down the river: "With permission I will take Fort Henry on the Tennessee and hold and establish a large camp there." Grant had made the same suggestion only a week before and been denied, during a rare face to face meeting with Halleck, but with the war order hanging over the heads of the general staff, Halleck was forced to reconsider his refusal. He did not believe that the maneuver Grant was suggesting could be carried off with less than 60,000 men, and Grant had fewer than 20,000. Nonetheless, Halleck gave his assent: "Make your preparations to take and hold Ft. Henry," he cabled back to Grant two days later. He also warned Grant that P.G.T. Beauregard, who had led the Confederate assault on Ft.

Sumter and commanded the southern forces at Bull Run, was advancing on his position with fifteen regiments of Confederate reinforcements. In other words, Grant would have to hurry if he was going to have any chance of success. "You will move with the least possible delay," Halleck told him.

By February 3, 1862, Grant was ready to launch "the great Union offensive in the West". It took only three days for Grant to get his forces back into fighting readiness, with all the attention to detail that a former quartermaster could supply. As Halleck nervously prepared to reinforce Grant in case anything went wrong, Grant managed to get within eight miles of Ft. Henry under the cover of a blustery winter night without Confederate spies getting wind of his movements. Compared to Columbus, now a heavily fortified Confederate stronghold, Ft. Henry was nothing but vulnerable to a potential enemy assault. It had been built hastily, on a flood plane, shortly after Tennessee seceded from the Union; worse than this, there were neither men nor guns enough to hold it. The best guns available in the fortress had last been used in the War of 1812. Ft. Henry's principle utility to the Confederates was that it was located very close to Ft. Donelson, which commanded access to the Cumberland River. Unlike Ft. Henry, Ft. Donelson was well manned and well supplied with munitions. Grant's forces vastly outnumbered the Ft. Henry garrison, but the Confederate forces amassed at Ft. Donelson were equal to Grant's, and entrenched besides.

Intelligence on both sides was poor. The garrison at Ft. Henry did not know Grant's men were approaching until they became visible from the river, while Grant did not know anything about the size of the Confederate garrison inside. But with a flotilla of gunships reinforcing his 15,000 men, swift victory was assured. The attack began at 11 a.m. on February 6, and was over by 3 p.m., when Grant wired Halleck that "Fort Henry is ours." Inspired by success, he indicated his intention to proceed to Ft. Donelson on February 8. Grant did not ask Halleck's permission for this second attack; emboldened by Lincoln's desire for forward momentum, he merely notified his superior of what was to come.

The Confederate officer who oversaw the surrender of Ft. Henry later wrote of his encounter with Grant, referring to him as "a modest, amiable, kind-hearted but resolute man." He went on to describe an encounter in which Grant intervened to save him from the wrath of a Union officer:

"While we were at headquarters an officer came in to report that he had not as yet found any papers giving information about our forces, and, to save him further looking, I informed him that I had destroyed all the papers bearing on the subject, at which he seemed very wroth, fussily demanding, 'By what authority?' Did I not know that I laid myself open to punishment, etc., etc. Before I could reply fully, General Grant quietly broke in with, 'I would be very much surprised and mortified if one of my subordinate officers should allow information which he could destroy to fall into the hands of the enemy.'"

Grant's victory at Ft. Donelson was not nearly so swift as his victory at Ft. Henry, and it was only made possible because Halleck had been quietly preparing reinforcements, should Grant need them, ever since Grant's departure. Beauregard, in conference with other Confederate generals, had decided that the best hope for retaining Confederate supremacy over the Tennessee River was to concentrate the might and main of their forces at Ft. Donelson, to crush Grant's command beyond the point of recovery. Beauregard was notoriously flashy and daring, and his colleagues were not entirely convinced of the wisdom of his plan. At first, it was decided that General Johnston would leave a small portion of his forces at Ft. Donelson in order to delay Grant's pursuit, and move the bulk of his army to Memphis. It would mean surrendering Kentucky and most of Tennessee to the Union, which would have a deleterious effect on Confederate morale, but it would keep a large portion of the army intact should Ft. Donelson fall. But at the last moment, Johnston changed his mind and chose to reinforce the fort's garrison. It would prove a disastrous decision.

"The nature of Grant's greatness has been a riddle to many observers," writes one biographer. "The evidence begins with the assault on Fort Donelson. Grant did not hedge his bets but on his own authority moved immediately against an enemy occupying a powerful fortified position. In so doing he disregarded explicit instructions to entrench at Fort Henry, ignored Halleck's order to prepare to receive a Confederate attack, and took virtually all of his command with him. Grant was in the heart of enemy country, facing a hostile force at least as large as his own, with nothing to fall back on in case of disaster. He was violating every maxim held dear by the military profession." But Grant's lack of military orthodoxy was inspired by his practical thinking. At West Point, one of his worst subjects had been tactics, but that was because he did not possess the imagination of a man like Halleck, who could envision a multiplicity of scenarios in advance of a battle from behind a desk. Rather, Grant's talent was for planting his boots on the field of battle, surveying the lay of the land, and letting the field itself teach him the tactics necessary for victory.

The siege of Ft. Donelson began on February 13. Generals George McClernand and George Ferguson Smith began probing for weaknesses along the Confederate line, only to meet with heavy casualties. On February 14, the Union flotilla commanded by Flag Officer Andrew H. Foote was repulsed by the heavy guns defending the fort. The pilothouse of the Union flagship *St. Louis* was hit by a direct blow from the Confederate guns, killing the pilot and wounding Foote in the ankle. The next shot destroyed the steering mechanism, and the crew of the *St. Louis* lost control of the ship, which drifted downriver. This constituted a heavy loss for Grant, who chose not to immediately inform Halleck, but he was not entirely discouraged; in a letter to Julia, he wrote, "The taking of Fort Donelson bids fair to be a long job. The rebels are strongly fortified and are in very heavy force. When this is to end is hard to surmise but I feel confident of ultimate success."

The next day, the Confederate commanders inside Ft. Donelson—John B. Floyd, Gideon Pillow, and Simon Bolivar Buckner—held a council of war in which they attempted to come to a consensus as to their next move. It was difficult to arrive at any consensus. The victory over the Union gunships had lifted their spirits, but the odds against them still seemed overwhelming—in part because they had drastically over-estimated the size of the Union force outside their walls. Only two choices lay before them: hold their position and pray that reinforcements arrived soon, or fight their way through the Union line and join the Confederate force encamped in Nashville. General Albert Sidney Johnston, Halleck's Confederate counterpart, had no good advice for his besieged commanders. After some debate, Floyd, Pillow, and Buckner agreed to fight their way out.

The breakout attack by the Confederate forces took Grant by surprise. He had ridden some seven miles away from the Union camp to confer with Foote aboard the *St. Louis*. Ordinarily Grant would not have left the field for any reason, but he trusted that Foote had good reasons for asking for the meeting, and Foote was unable to come to him due to the injuries he had received the previous day. When Grant returned, having given Foote permission to take his two most heavily damaged ships back to Cairo for repairs, he was met with the news that a three-pronged Confederate attack was underway, and the McClernand's division had been overcome and driven into a retreat.

Grant had a number of talents which made him an admirable general, but on that particular afternoon it was his prodigious horsemanship which turned the tide of the battle, and arguably the war. Across frozen fields, he galloped the seven miles back to the front lines, where he assumed personal command of the men fighting in the field. There, he discovered that McClernand's division had taken heavy losses and that the men were standing around with no orders to follow and no ammunition left in their haversacks. But Grant's presence quickly rallied them again. "Fill your cartridge boxes quick, and get into line," he told them. "The enemy is trying to escape and he must not be permitted to do." The men, who were still eager to fight and only waiting for instructions, hastened to obey.

The discord between the three Confederate commanders inside Ft. Donelson had worked to Grant's advantage. Pillow, Floyd, and Buckner had each issued different instructions to their men as to what their next move ought to be after they had broken through the Union line. Pillow had told his men to return to Ft. Donelson to pack up their gear before they headed on to Nashville, which was why the men of McClernand's division had not been captured or run to ground and were instead standing around aimlessly, waiting for Grant to give them new orders. Buckner had ordered his division to be prepared to ride straight on for Nashville after breaking out of the fort, while Floyd, the least experienced of the three, had neglected to make a decision either way. Pillow, believing that his rout of McClernand's division had amounted to a complete victory over the Union forces, countermanded Buckner's orders to march for Nashville, instead ordering his men to load the supply wagons and retrieve the fort's guns. This provided Grant's men with the opportunity to seize control of the road to Nashville, cutting of their escape route.

Charles Ferguson Smith, technically outranked by Grant, was many years older than him, and had in fact been one of Grant's instructors at West Point. As such, Grant looked upon him more as a mentor than a subordinate. Smith was, like Grant, the sort of soldier who looked for every opportunity to force open battle, so it was without hesitation that Grant issued Smith his orders: "General Smith," he said, "all has failed to our right. You must take Fort Donelson." Smith's reply was equally to the point. "I will do it, General," he said, and immediately began to prepare his troop of volunteers to seize the fort in a bayonet charge. By the standards of the hesitant tactics being employed in the early days of the Civil War, this was a move of unprecedented daring. Smith arranged his regiments in a column, positioned himself at its head, and led the charge, "down the steep side of the ravine, through underbrush 'too thick for a rabbit to get through', across a small stream at the bottom, and up the opposite slope into the rebel abatis." Although Buckner arrived to reinforce the fort, it was too late. By 4 p.m.— three hours after Grant arrived back in camp to learn of the Confederate breakout—the battle was over. The surviving Confederates returned to the fort to tend their wounded, while Grant returned to his command post. Along the way, Grant noticed that amongst the piles of dead bodies, a wounded Union soldier lay next to a wounded Confederate soldier. The Union soldier was attempting to give the Confederate a drink of water. Grant asked for a flask, gave both men a swallow of brandy, then ordered them carried away on stretchers. When the Union orderlies left the Confederate soldier where he was, Grant ordered them to return for him. "Take the Confederate too," he said. "The war is over between them."

In the comparative safety of Ft. Donelson, the Confederate commanders, after an acrimonious and heated discussion, decided that surrender was their only option. They still believed that the Union forces arrayed against them were twice as numerous as they actually were, and they concluded that at least three-quarters of the men under their command would die if they attempted to break for Nashville again. No commander, they felt, "had the right to make such a sacrifice of human life." All that was left to decide was who would offer the surrender. According to a biographer of Gideon Pillow, the dialogue between the three commanders in Ft. Donelson on the night of February 16, 1862, went as follows:

"I turn the command over, sir," Floyd told Pillow.

"I pass it," Pillow told Buckner.

"I assume it," said Buckner. "Give me pen, ink, and paper, and send for a bugler."

It fell to Buckner to offer the surrender of Ft. Donelson to Grant. Buckner knew Grant well; a few years earlier, when an impoverished and dispirited Grant was stranded in New York after resigning his commission in the army, Buckner had encountered him by chance and offered his assistance by guaranteeing his hotel bills. He knew that Grant was a man of honor, so he did not fear for the lives of his men. "In consideration of all circumstances governing the present situation of affairs at this station," Buckner wrote to Grant, "I propose to the commanding officers of the Federal forces the appointment of commissioners to agree upon terms of capitulation of the forces and post under my command, and in that view suggest an armistice until 12 o'clock today."

This message was carried by a Confederate officer under a flag of truce until it reached Charles Ferguson Smith, who promptly relayed it to Grant. Grant, unaware of the drama that had lately ensued in the command room at Ft. Donelson, was confused to be receiving a message from Buckner rather than Pillow or Floyd. He asked Smith what the response ought to be. "No terms with the damned rebels," came the reply from Smith, which made Grant laugh. He then took up a pen and wrote a reply which one biographer refers to as "one of the most famous dispatches in the history of warfare":

"Sir: Yours of this date proposing Armistice and appointment of Commissioners to settle terms of Capitulation is just received. No terms except complete and unconditional surrender can be accepted. I propose to move immediately upon your works. I am, sir, very respectfully, Your obt. svt., U.S. Grant, Brig. Gen."

Buckner was stunned by Grant's reply, for two reasons. The first was that he believed the personal friendship he had enjoyed with Grant entitled him to more generous terms. The second had to do with the attitude which, up to that point, had prevailed amongst the high command of both the Union and Confederate armies. Part of the reason why so little progress was made during the first two years of the war was because both Union and Confederate generals saw the war as a conflict between gentlemen, to be conducted along ancient, outdated modes of chivalry. It was this attitude which so frustrated Lincoln and which led Buckner to expect that Grant would honor his offer to discuss terms of surrender in a leisurely, civilized manner. For Grant to declare openly and unapologetically that he intended to press his advantage against an enemy which had frankly admitted its weakness and inability to continue the fight was completely contrary to the style of warfare that had been taught at West Point. But Grant, like his friend William Tecumseh Sherman, believed that the only merciful war was a short war, and the only way to make a war shorter was to crush the enemy until it could not fight back. Allowing the garrison at Ft. Donelson to retreat in an orderly fashion only to join up with the Confederate forces in Nashville would only prolong the war and raise the death toll. By announcing his intention to crush the rebels in Ft. Donelson regardless of their willingness to entertain the prospect of surrendering, Grant was changing the rules of engagement.

Buckner's reply to Grant made no attempt to mask his feelings over the brusqueness of the general's answer: "The overwhelming force under your command, compels me, notwithstanding the brilliant success of the

Confederate armies yesterday, to accept the ungenerous and unchivalrous terms which you propose." Nonetheless, when Grant actually arrived to meet with the Confederate commanders, he and Buckner soon re-established their old harmonious rapport. Grant gave Buckner permission for the Confederates to gather and bury their dead, and promised to supplement their dwindling food stores from the Union commissary. Officers and enlisted men alike were permitted to keep their personal possessions. Grant was not without chivalry—but he would be chivalrous on his own terms.

All across the Union, people celebrated their first major, decisive victory of the war. Halleck recommended to George McClellan that Pope, Buell, and Grant be made major generals; Secretary of War Edwin Stanton passed only a third of that recommendation on to Lincoln, who took special pride in granting the promotion to Grant, because he, like Lincoln, was lately of

Illinois. The capture of Ft. Donelson was the greatest American victory since the Battle of Yorktown in the Revolutionary War. This, combined with the speed with which Grant had taken Ft. Henry and Ft. Donelson, were sufficient to establish him as a legend. Thanks to him, Kentucky and Tennessee were secured for the Union, and the heart of the Confederacy was vulnerable to Union incursion. And perhaps most importantly at all, the critical Union victory devastated any chance that the Confederacy had of securing assistance or allies from Europe. Ft. Donelson sent a message abroad—the civil war in America was a purely domestic affair that would eventually be set to rights by the legitimate government of the country. Interference was not necessary.

# Chapter Four: Shiloh and Vicksburg

## Shiloh

After his extraordinary victory at Ft. Donelson, Grant was a hero in the eyes of the public and his value had become apparent to persons such as Edwin Stanton and Abraham Lincoln. But his relationship with Halleck, his direct superior, suffered. Communication lines broke down between Grant at Ft. Henry and Halleck in St. Louis for over two weeks; during that time Halleck sent repeated requests for Grant to submit after-action reports stating his casualty count, the strength of the army after the battle, and other routine facts that were necessary for the further planning of the war. Grant, who never received these requests, nonetheless wrote to Halleck between one and three times a day with fresh reports regarding the state of his army. He was, therefore, bewildered when an angry letter from Halleck finally reached him, demanding that he account for his silence. A series of further miscommunications occurred, until Halleck at last began to receive the reports from Grant that had been delayed by the mail wagons. But by then, Grant was irate over what seemed to him terribly unjust treatment, coming from a man whom he had always admired without reservation. He forwarded copies of Halleck's rebuking letter, and his own reply—in which he asked to be relieved of his command—to Washington, where it came to the attention of his original patron, Congressman Elihu Washburne, who immediately brought it to Lincoln's attention. By this time, Grant could do little wrong in Lincoln's eyes, and the next communication which Halleck received from Washington conveyed a clear message: if he wanted to make complaints about Grant, those complaints had better be serious, and backed up by incontrovertible proofs.

Halleck, who had grown envious of Grant's fame after his victory at Ft. Donelson, felt obligated to write another, more soothing letter to Grant. Halleck informed him that it was impossible to relieve him of command. In fact, he told Grant that he was to assume command of a new army: the Army of the Tennessee, consisting of five divisions. The 1st division was led by George McClernand; the 2nd by Charles Ferguson Smith; the 3rd by Lew Wallace; the 4th by Brigadier General Stephen A. Hurlbut; and the 5th by William Sherman. The 1st, 2nd, and 3rd divisions were composed of veterans, experienced soldiers who had been present at Ft. Donelson or other battles. The 4th and 5th divisions were new and untested. The army's purpose was to drive the remaining Confederate forces out of Tennessee permanently. Shortly after assuming command of the Army of the Tennessee, Grant ordered the 4th and 5th divisions to make camp near the town of Corinth, where the Confederates were maintaining position, while the 1st and 2nd divisions were ordered to a site called Pittsburg

Landing, on the advice of General Sherman. Pittsburg Landing was a short march from Corinth, and provided space to command the Tennessee River from both banks.

Grant, unsurprisingly, wished to prepare for an immediate assault on the Confederates at Corinth. His forces numbered 45,000; the Confederates numbered around 40,000. Grant had never been afraid of fighting a battle of equal odds. But Halleck, like most high ranking Union generals, preferred not to engage the enemy until the odds were overwhelmingly in his favor. It was typical in the early years of the Civil War for generals like Halleck and McClellan to delay battles so that green, untried troops could be drilled to perfection, and reinforcements in the tens of thousands could make their way slowly overland to the projected battle site. Grant had no patience for this approach; delaying battle in order to drill green troops only gave the enemy the same opportunity to drill theirs, and in the mean time, any advantage of surprise was lost. But Halleck ordered him to hold off on striking at Corinth until 25,000 troops under the command of Don Carlos Buell arrived to reinforce him. Grant, having no choice but to follow orders, concentrated on drilling the inexperienced troops of the 4th and 5th divisions, and creating a 6th division to his army under the command of Brigadier General Benjamin Prentiss.

Halleck soon received intelligence which indicated to him that the Confederates were abandoning Corinth. He wired orders to Grant that he was to move in quickly and destroy the railroad that was located there. Grant was perfectly willing to do this. Contrary to the report Halleck had received, the Confederates had not deserted Corinth, and Grant knew it. But he was eager to seize the opportunity of attacking them, and Halleck's order to destroy the railroad gave him cover to do so without defying his previous order. But Halleck, by now accustomed to Grant's opportunistic approach to battle, wired back, re-asserting that he was not to divide his forces until Buell's reinforcements had arrived. This was deeply frustrating to Grant, who could only surmise that the Confederates were also likely to be reinforced while he waited for Buell's troops to march the one hundred and forty miles to Pittsburg Landing. "I do not hear one word from St. Louis," Grant groused to Charles Ferguson Smith. "I am clearly of the opinion that the enemy are gathering strength at Corinth quite as rapidly as we are here, and the sooner we attack the easier will be the task of taking the place."

The Confederate cause was forced into desperate measures by the defeat at Ft. Donelson, and, as if taking their cue from Grant's shocking "unconditional surrender" terms, General Albert Sydney Johnston took advantage of the Union delay to launch a surprise attack. Much as Grant would have preferred to attack Corinth without delay, he was only frustrated by Halleck's orders, not concerned that his army was in any serious danger. He later wrote that "I regarded the campaign we were engaged in an offensive one and had no idea that the enemy would leave strong entrenchments to take the initiative when he knew he would be attacked where he was if he remained."

On April 3, 1862, Johnston, commanding the Army of the Mississippi, ordered his forces to advance on Pittsburg Landing, where Grant, none the wiser, was impatiently awaiting reinforcements. Johnston's army numbered around 44,000 men, making it the largest force the Confederate army had ever mounted before a battle. However, most of the Confederate army were new volunteers, compared to Grant's army, which was half composed of the veterans of Ft. Donelson. And thanks to Grant's background as a quartermaster, his troops were, as ever, better fed and better supplied than any army then fighting. But the Confederates were spurred on by the knowledge that the upcoming battle might end the war, and not in their favor. "You can but march to decisive victory over the agrarian mercenaries sent to subjugate you and despoil you of your liberties, property, and honor," Johnston told his soldiers on the eve of battle. "Remember the dependence of your mothers, your wives, your sisters, and your children on the result; remember the fair, broad, abounding land, the happy homes and the ties that would be desolated by your defeat. The eyes and hopes of eight millions of people rest upon you."

When Johnston at last struck, Grant, Sherman, Smith, and the rest of the Union commanders were caught with their pants down. Sherman had been warned by one of his own scouts that Confederate infantry had been spotted in the woods, but Sherman had angrily informed him that "Beauregard is not such a fool as to leave his base of operations and attack us in ours." If Grant, Smith, and Sherman had strengths which other Union generals lacked, namely the desire to force confrontations with the enemy whenever feasible, they also shared a common blind spot— they never seemed to anticipate the possibility that the enemy might take a page from their own book and show the initiative. Protected by this blindness in his enemies, Johnston's armies marched 23 miles away from Corinth and descended on five divisions of Grant's army at Pittsburg Landing on April 6, 1862.

Civil War historian Jean Edward Smith writes that,

"Johnston delegated to Beauregard the task of drawing the attack plan and that may have been his first mistake. Known as Special Orders No. 8, it was modeled on Napoleon's blueprint for the battle of Waterloo. Common sense suggests

Beauregard should have recalled what happened to Napoleon at Waterloo, but like most West Pointers he was mesmerized by the military reputation of the emperor. (Curiously, the stodgy tenacity of the Duke of Wellington never excited much respect at West Point, although it was exactly this trait in Grant that prevailed at Shiloh."

In other words, rather than ranging his divisions side by side, which would have crushed the unprepared Union forces, Beauregard chose to stack them in a column, one behind the other. Beauregard envisioned that the endless line of soldiers descending on the Union camp would be as devastating as "an Alpine avalanche". However, there are numerous problems with such an arrangement, one of them being that only the soldiers at the front of the column could fire their guns at the enemy—everyone else ran the risk of shooting their own men in the backs. Furthermore, it took so long to get the immense column moving that instead of attacking promptly at sunrise, which had been the plan, the Confederates showed up 90 minutes behind schedule—90 minutes of broad daylight that permitted Benjamin Prentiss to see them coming and sound the alarm.

The surprise attack was successful, at first. Prentiss's command, the newly created 6th division of the Army of the Tennessee, was effectively wiped out. But Sherman's veteran division fared better, and managed to retreat to high ground, near a small church called Shiloh, "named by early Methodist settlers for the Israelite shrine established by Joshua after the conquest of the land of Canaan." Sherman managed to hold his ground under three separate Confederate charges. Grant, who had been felled with a serious ankle injury a few days before when his horse lost its footing in soft ground and rolled on him, was late arriving to the field, but he assumed immediate command, riding into battle with a crutch strapped across his saddle in case he had to dismount.

Having successfully routed a division of Grant's army, Johnston's soldiers, like the volunteer Union soldiers after Belmont, lost unit cohesion and began to celebrate their victory. Unlike Grant's army, they were hungry and not well supplied, and the fact that they had just taken possession of a camp where breakfast could still be found hot on the cook fires was too great a temptation to resist. It took an hour for Confederate commanders to regain control of their men, an hour that Grant used to good advantage, reforming his line under cover. Once Johnston's men were ready to fight again, he drove them towards the west, where William Sherman's division was still repulsing the Confederate onslaught. Grant took advantage of the opportunity to re-establish his forces at Pittsburg Landing, along the banks of the Tennessee River, even though the whole purpose of the Confederate attack had been to drive him far away from it. This done, Grant rode out to Sherman's position. Sherman had been wounded twice and had three horses shot out from under him, but he was unperturbed. Grant told him to hold position, as three reinforcement divisions would soon join them.

By mid-morning, three of Grant's remaining five divisions had been captured, but Beauregard's battle plan had not survived contact with the enemy. The central Union line was holding. When Buell at last arrived with his reinforcements, the situation appeared so bleak to him that he asked Grant what preparations he had made for a retreat in the morning. Grant informed him that he had no intention of retreating: "I haven't despaired of whipping them yet," he told Buell.

A disastrous piece of bad luck struck the Confederate army at the very moment Grant was dismissing Buell's assumption that retreat was necessary. General Albert Sydney Johnston was struck in the leg by a minié ball, severing an artery. He bled out swiftly and died. Though Johnston was nominally the highest ranking Confederate officer in the field—indeed, he was the highest ranking officer on either side of the conflict to be killed during the war—P.G.T. Beauregard was the mind behind the Confederate attack plan. When he learned that Johnston was dead, he switched gears and began attempting to drive Grant's line away from the river. The fighting at the center of the conflict—called "the hornet's nest" by the men fighting there—became so intense, with such immense casualties, that the living had to scramble over the bodies of the dead to reach the enemy. Grant later wrote that the ground was "so covered with dead that it would have been possible to walk across, in any direction, stepping on dead bodies, without a foot touching the ground."

When the day's fighting ended at nightfall, Beauregard was convinced that Confederate victory was assured. Grant, by contrast, was overheard by an aide muttering, "Not beaten yet, not by a damn sight," as he looked over the battle lines. The casualties were immense—over ten thousand Union soldiers had been killed or captured, while almost the same number were too rattled by the twelve hours of vicious fighting to do much of anything except mill about and reassure themselves that they were still alive. Grant's line, though unbroken, had been pushed back two miles from its original position. Two of his divisions had been wiped out; one of his commanders, Wallace, was missing, while Benjamin Prentiss had been taken prisoner. But Grant was already planning his dawn counterattack. He informed his nervous officers that he intended to use the fresh reinforcements which had recently arrived with Buell to drive the Confederates back to Corinth. "So confident was I," he later wrote, "that the next day would bring victory if we could only take the initiative that I directed [each of his division commanders] to throw out heavy lines of skirmishers in the morning as soon as they could see, and push them forward until they found the enemy, following with their entire division, and to engage the enemy as soon as found."

By that point, Grant was the only man in the Union army with any optimism left—even Sherman, having labored for five hours to get his division back into fighting readiness, thought that retreat was their only option. But when he approached Grant to discuss it, he found him leaning against an oak tree in the rain with a cigar clamped between his lips, and "moved...by some wise and sudden instinct not to mention retreat", Sherman merely said, "Well, Grant, we've had the devil's own day, haven't we?" To which Grant replied, "Yes. Lick 'em tomorrow though."

During the night, as thousands of Union reinforcements arrived under the cover of darkness, Confederate general Nathan Bedford Forrest reported the movements to one of Beauregard's subordinates, who dismissed the activity Forrest had noticed as a retreat. The Confederate commanders, to a man, were convinced that the Union army would make easy pickings the next day. But Grant retained an advantage that Beauregard did not have. Because Beauregard had arrayed his troop divisions in a column, instead of side by side, during the initial assault, the divisions had become hopelessly intermingled. This meant that soldiers became separated from the other men in their divisions, and from their commanding officers. It would be impossible to command the army to best advantage, until the divisions had been reorganized. Beauregard and his division commanders were aware of the problem, but confident in their victory, they elected to wait until first light to put the divisions back in order. Grant's men, by contrast, were still organized in their original divisions. Though casualties had been approximately equal in both the Union and Confederate armies, 30,000 disorganized soldiers would fall easily under an organized attack by 30,000 soldiers maintaining discipline and order—as Beauregard was to learn to his cost.

In accordance with Grant's orders that the division commanders have their men ready to move at first light, preparations for the Union counterattack began at 3 a.m., and by 5 a.m. the line was advancing. By now, the Union army numbered 40,000, over half of which were new reinforcements, fresh, rested, unwounded, and eager for their crack at the enemy. What followed was virtually a repeat of the previous day's attack, only with the Confederate and Union positions reversed. This time it was the Confederates who were caught by surprise—not

90 minutes after dawn, but in the dim blue light of dawn itself. By two in the afternoon, one of Beauregard's officers advised retreat: "General, do you not think our troops in the condition of a lump of sugar thoroughly soaked with water, but yet preserving its original shape, though ready to dissolve?" The truth of his observation was manifest, and Beauregard ordered the retreat to Corinth. Having regained the contested battlefield, Grant did not have the heart to order his men to pursue the Confederates in retreat. His army had been victorious, but it was unclear to him what had been gained. The battle of Shiloh forced Grant to think of the entire war in a new light. Up to that point, everyone—soldiers, officers, generals, Confederate, Union—had believed that the conflict between the north and the south would be short-lived, the outcome determined by one or two decisive battles. Now, Grant realized, the Confederacy would not surrender, no matter how heavy their losses, until their army was crushed entirely. He wrote in his memoirs,

"Up to that time it had been the policy of our army, certainly of that portion commanded by me, to protect the property of citizens whose territory was invaded, without regard to its sentiments, whether Union or Secession. After this, I regarded it as humane to both sides to protect the persons of those found at their homes, but to consume everything that could be used to support or supply armies...I continued this policy to the close of the war."

Historians estimate that the number of people who died at the battle of Shiloh were greater than the total number of Americans who died in the Revolutionary War and the Mexican-American War combined. But the Union victory at Shiloh had made the chances of Confederate victory considerably more remote than they had been at the war's outset. The great southern advantage in the western frontier was gone. Shiloh, like Ft. Donelson, was celebrated as a tremendous victory in Union newspapers, and Grant was once again a hero—until the casualty lists were reported. After that, there was a sudden and furious backlash against Grant, who was once again tarnished by the old rumors that he had a severe drinking problem, the implication being that he had been caught unawares at Shiloh because he was drunk. Lincoln, however, turned a deaf ear to those who implored him to remove Grant from command. "I can't spare this man," Lincoln declared. "He fights."

## Vicksburg

After Shiloh, Halleck came to Pittsburg Landing to take personal command of the combined army Grant had led into battle. Unaccustomed to commanding such large numbers of soldiers, Halleck retained Grant as his second in command, just in case any fresh fighting should break out. But as the lull between battles stretched on, it became evident that Grant was miserably unsuited for his new role. Always before, even when he was a mere lieutenant and quartermaster, he had been a commander; as Halleck's deputy, his role was to advise and support the commander. Grant lacked the temperament and the patience needed for such work. Soon, he succumbed to a despair similar to that which had plagued him in California. Once again, he did not have enough to do, and once again, he began to seriously consider the possibility of resigning his commission and returning to his family. It was Sherman who talked him out of it. He pointed out that the war would go on with or without Grant, but if he left, Grant "could not be quiet at home for a week when armies were moving". If he stayed, however, Halleck, or someone in Washington, might finally decide to let Grant return to the battlefield. Grant wrote to his wife that very evening to tell her that he would not be coming home after all: "necessity changes my plans, or the public service does, and I must yield."

After Shiloh, Halleck had declined to pursue the defeated Confederate army to Corinth and crush them there, though it would have been a comparatively easy task. This was because crippling the Confederate army through open battle was not his objective. "There is no point in bringing on a battle if the object can be obtained without one," he wrote. "I think that by showing a bold front for a day or two the enemy will continue his retreat, which is all that I desire." No philosophy could be more contrary to Grant's own, but Halleck, like other West Point commanders of the wait-and-see school, believed that a war skillfully waged was a war in which scarcely any fighting took place at all. Victory, in his view, was achieved by gaining control of key strategic locations, such as Corinth—and Vicksburg, Mississippi, the last Confederate stronghold commanding access to the Mississippi River.

It was Corinth that mattered to Halleck, not the Confederate army that was occupying it. He did not order an attack against Beauregard's army at Corinth until scouts reported that it seemed as if the town was mobilizing for another assault against Union forces. What the scouts had actually observed were preparations for a mass evacuation of the town. Beauregard's entire army, including all their supplies, guns, and munitions, had been spirited away to Nashville by rail in the night. Even the townspeople had gone with them—of all the families that had been living in Corinth, only two remained behind. Despite Grant's victory at Shiloh, Corinth had, ultimately, not been taken from the Confederates—the Confederates had stripped it bare, then given it to them, "compliments of P.G.T. Beauregard". Halleck was just as pleased to have come into possession of the town, and its rail line, without loss of life, but Grant was profoundly irritated that he had missed an opportunity to capture guns and munitions. Had Grant been allowed to pursue Beauregard as he wished, he would have been able to "deliver a knockout blow", as one historian puts it. Instead, the fighting would continue for another two years.

Eventually, Halleck broke up the combined army that fought at Shiloh and placed Grant back in command of the Army of the Tennessee. The veterans of Shiloh were now an army of occupation, cooling their heels at a number of scattered rail stops along the border of Mississippi and Tennessee. Shortly afterwards, Halleck was summoned to Washington to replace George McClellan as general in chief of the Union forces; Grant thus succeeded Halleck to the command of a new army which combined Grant's old command with the armies previously commanded by John Pope. During the latter half of 1862, the Union suffered a series of embarrassing defeats, culminating in the narrow defeat of Robert E. Lee's Army of Northern Virginia by McClellan's Army of the Potomac at Antietam. The Union victory at Antietam effectively repulsed the Confederate onslaught into the heart of federal territory—Washington, Baltimore, and the Potomac region. Immediately after Antietam, Abraham Lincoln issued the Emancipation Proclamation, which designated that, effective on the first day of the new year, "all persons held as slaves within any State or designated part of a State, the people whereof shall then be in rebellion against the United States" would be free under federal law. The slaves held in the border states, which were still loyal to the Union, would not be liberated until the passage of the Thirteenth Amendment. Lincoln had been sitting on the proclamation for several months, but he ha wanted to wait for a decisive Union victory before announcing it, lest it be said that he was stripping the rebels of their slaves in order to strike at them with the pen after the sword had proven too dull for the job.

With Halleck no longer looking over his shoulder, Grant decided to concentrate his forces and begin an offensive against Vicksburg. Grant did not subscribe to Halleck's "places" theory of war, but he understood the importance of Vicksburg. In the 19th century, waterways in general were of crucial importance to the movement of men, munitions, and supplies, because it was much faster and safer for an army to travel by boat than to travel overland. The Mississippi in particular was the most strategically important waterway in the south. The Confederate army, having traveled north to strike at Union strongholds and keep the fighting away from their homes, was separated from the southern heartland by many hundreds of miles. In order to feed itself, the army depended on its westernmost states: Texas, which provided beef, Louisiana, which supplied sugar, salt, and molasses, and Missouri, which supplied lead for bullets. But if the Confederacy lost control of the river, then Louisiana would find itself cut off from Mississippi, Arkansas from Tennessee, Missouri from Illinois, and Kentucky from Indiana and Ohio.

After the battle of Shiloh, the last section of the Mississippi river that remained under Confederate control was the section between Vicksburg, Mississippi, and Port Hudson, Louisiana. All supplies traveling east to supply the southern armies passed through the Vicksburg rail line. Lieutenant General John Pemberton, a Pennsylvanian who had joined the cause of secession at the behest of his Virginia-born wife, was in charge of defending both Vicksburg and Port Hudson. He had little combat experience and the defenses at Vicksburg were considered light. But Confederate president Jefferson Davis charged him to defend Vicksburg at all costs, referring to the town as "the nail

head that holds the South's two halves together".
Davis, a West Pointer like Halleck, also
subscribed to the places theory of war.

Unbeknownst to Grant, his second in command,
John McClernand, a man Grant had never
entirely trusted due to his poorly concealed
political ambitions, was agitating his longtime
friend Lincoln to authorize a separate,
independent attack on Vicksburg. Lincoln
granted this authorization without informing
Grant, but Halleck, who often had his differences
with Grant but was too appreciative of Grant's
abilities to permit a loose cannon like
McClernand to interfere with his command,
made certain that language was inserted in
McClernand's order that made him subordinate
to Grant in the field. Grant was satisfied with this
arrangement, but less satisfied in the knowledge
that McClernand outranked Sherman, Grant's
right hand. It was necessary to keep Sherman
and his command out of McClernand's reach, or

Sherman was likely to find himself taking orders from a man who cared little for Grant's strategies. Grant ordered Sherman to move all Union troops along the Mississippi "down the river to the vicinity of Vicksburg, and with the cooperation of the gunboat fleet under command of Flag-officer Porter, proceed to the reduction of that place in such manner as circumstances, and your own judgment, may dictate." Sherman was well away from Memphis on his way to Vicksburg by the time McClernand showed up in Memphis to assume command.

The Vicksburg campaign lasted for several months and consisted of a two-pronged maneuver, or series of maneuvers, in which Grant attempted to lure the Confederate garrison out from behind its fortifications, while William Sherman's divisions took the city in a surprise attack. But the diversionary tactic failed; Confederate forces, led by Nathan Bedford Forrest and Earl Van Dorn, pursued Grant doggedly and destroyed his supply lines, forcing him back long enough for Confederate reinforcements to arrive by rail to defend Vicksburg. Forrest destroyed the majority of the telegraph lines in the area, so Grant could not warn Sherman, who was preparing to attack Vicksburg's defenses, that Pemberton's army was waiting for him. As a result, Sherman, launching four divisions of his army against the defenses on Chickasaw Bluffs, found the battlements manned, and his soldiers coming under heavy fire. He was repulsed, with heavy casualties. "Our loss has been heavy," he noted later, "and we accomplished nothing." Sherman retreated upriver; the winter portion of the Vicksburg campaign was over.

In the late winter of 1862, McClernand caught up with Sherman in the wake of his defeat at Chickasaw Bluffs and assumed command of his forces. After McClernand, apparently in an attempt to raise morale, led a series of pointless attacks against minor Confederate outposts, Grant complained to Halleck, who immediately removed McClernand and restored command of his so-called Army of the Mississippi to Grant. With McClernand out of the way, Grant changed tactics, abandoning his overland campaign to embark on the greatest amphibious assault yet seen in American military history. By this point, Union morale was at an all time low; there were no longer enough new volunteers joining up, so a draft had to be instated. Worse yet, Lincoln's chances of winning re-election in 1864 looked grim, unless a decisive Union victory came to the rescue of his reputation. Sherman had already demonstrated that a direct assault on the natural bluffs protecting Vicksburg would be ineffective; not unlike a medieval castle surrounded by a moat, Vicksburg was well equipped with natural defenses that made it virtually impregnable. Grant's task was therefore to move around Vicksburg in order to besiege it from the high ground. While Grant was waiting for the ground, sodden with winter rains, to dry up in the spring, he confused and distracted the observing Confederates with a series of attempts to dig channels that would divert enough water flow from the Mississippi to provide him with way around Vicksburg, out of reach of its guns. It was little more than an exercise to pass the time and muddy the metaphorical waters—Grant had no great hopes of success—but in this case, it was more important to be seen doing something than to actually accomplish the apparent objective. It also kept his soldiers occupied, which was of crucial importance to their morale. Bored soldiers were more likely to desert than busy soldiers.

Grant tried, and failed, seven different times to flank Vicksburg's defenses, and the newspapers turned against him. Lincoln's advisers began repeating the old rumors about Grant's drinking habits and encouraging the president to replace him. "I think Grant has hardly a friend left, except myself," said Lincoln. "What I want, and what the people want, is generals who will fight battles and win victories. Grant has done this and I propose to stand by him." When a delegation of congressmen visited Lincoln to demand that Grant be removed from command because he was a drunkard, Lincoln "then began to ask them if they knew what he drank, what brand of whiskey he used, telling them seriously that I wished they could find out. They conferred with each other and concluded they could not tell me what brand he used. I urged them to ascertain and let me know, for if it made fighting generals like Grant, I should like to get some of it for distribution."

It seems as though Grant did take up drinking again during the Vicksburg campaign, but in a modest way. The Assistant Secretary of War, Charles Dana, who had been sent to Grant's camp by Edwin Stanton for the express purpose of monitoring Grant's drinking habits, reported that "General Grant's seasons of intoxication were not only infrequent, occurring once in three or four months, but he always chose a time when the gratification of his appetite for drink would not interfere with any important movement that had to be directed or attended to by him." Grant's moderation was due in part to his own awareness of that he was unusually susceptible to alcohol, and also due to the vigilance of his adjutant, Colonel John Rawlins, who made it his purpose to watch Grant's drinking and chastise him when appropriate. Casting aside deference to rank for the greater good, Rawlins wrote to Grant on one occasion that "The great solicitude I feel for the safety of this army leads me to mention what I had hoped never again to do— the subject of your drinking... I have heard that Dr. McMillan, at General Sherman's a few days ago, induced you...to take a glass of wine, and today, I found a case of wine in front of your tent, and tonight, when you should have been in bed, I find you where the wine bottle has just been emptied, in company of those who drink and urge you to do likewise. Lack of your usual promptness of decision and clearness in expressing yourself in writing tend to confirm my suspicion." Rawlins continued, telling Grant that he must not drink any longer, or "...no matter by whom asked or under what circumstances, let my immediate relief from duty in this department be the result." Rawlins would stay by Grant's side for the rest of the war and later accompany him to Washington, so it seems likely that this rebuke had the intended effect.

Whatever Grant's level of alcohol consumption, it was not responsible for his frustrations in the Vicksburg campaign. Even Halleck, now commanding the bird's eye view of the Union armies from Washington, came to appreciate the value of Grant's being the one general under his command who sought every opportunity to engage the enemy. Beginning in January of 1863, Grant concentrated on a plan that would enable him to "move south of the Confederate citadel, cut himself off from his supply base at Memphis, march east into Mississippi toward Jackson, turn 180 degrees and strike Vicksburg from the side on which it was vulnerable"—a move which one biographer refers to as "one of the great strategic gambits in modern warfare." All the canal digging he had ordered in the late winter and early spring was just biding his time until the plan gained cohesion. By late March, he knew what he had to do. First, McClernand's division was to build roads and repair bridges over muddy, flooded swamplands. Grant's men would use these roads to take possession of the town of New Carthage. From there, they would rendezvous with Admiral Porter, whose ironclad ships would run the Vicksburg gun battery to ferry Grant's army from the west bank of the river to the east. The biggest risk of the enterprise, apart from the danger to the ships, lay in the fact that Grant was cutting himself off from his own supply lines. But the former quartermaster had observed earlier that it was remarkably easy for his soldiers to live off the land they were traversing. Porter's first run was so successful, resulting in the loss of only one supply ship, that Grant ordered a second, and again, only one boat and a few barges were lost.

On April 30, 1863, once his troops had made landfall unopposed by Confederate forces, Grant found himself commanding 23,000 Union soldiers in Confederate territory. The rest of his forces, and Sherman's, soon followed. There, Sherman made a second charge against Chickasaw Bluffs, a strictly diversionary tactic to keep Pemberton's attention away from the main strength of Grant's army. Meanwhile, Grant launched a feint of his own, striking at Pemberton's supply line and tearing a swathe of destruction through central Mississippi. They destroyed rail lines and supply houses and burned buildings, tempting Pemberton's men into chasing them. A blitzkrieg inland campaign followed, culminating in the capture of the Mississippi capital of Jackson. In taking Jackson, Grant cut Pemberton's army off from the army of

General Joseph E. Johnston, and seized control of the railway that was supplying Vicksburg from the east.

It is an axiom of warfare that when an army is besieging a fortified location, they must outnumber the army inside it three to one. But it is also known that once a city under siege loses its ability to be resupplied, it is only a matter of time until starvation, not gunfire, will force a surrender. West Pointer that he was, Pemberton knew this well, yet it was still with the greatest reluctance that he obeyed General Johnston's orders to rendezvous with his army at nearby Clinton—and, in the process search out and destroy Grant's supply line. Neither Pemberton nor Johnston realized that Grant did not *have* a supply line. It would never in a million years have crossed their minds that a seasoned general like Grant would strike out on a venture that would make it impossible for his army to resupply itself. But Grant's army, living off the land, was eating better than they had eaten on military rations; there was abundant beef, greenery, strawberries, and other luxuries to be found in the surrounding countryside. Furthermore, when Grant captured Jackson, he also captured well-stocked Confederate larders that put an end to any shortages his army might have been facing. One soldier remarked that they "lived fat" and that if, as rumors indicated, the south was starving, there was certainly no sign of it where Grant's army was marching.

Once Grant's combined forces overpowered Pemberton's at the battle of Champion Hill, Vicksburg was as good as in Union hands. Grant's army was now between Pemberton and the city he was defending. Pemberton retreated to a fortified position he had prepared in advance, where the works were so formidable that Grant immediately decided not to attempt a frontal assault, but to wait for Sherman's men to catch up and reinforce them. Then, in what one observer called "the most perilous and ludicrous charge I witnessed during the war", one of Grant's officers, Brigadier General Michael Lawler, abruptly and without orders led McClernand's troops in a charge on the Confederate position. Grant, whose genius lay in his ability to adapt to a battlefield that was constantly in flux, immediately joined the charge with the entire Union line behind him. Pemberton lost 1800 men and eighteen pieces of artillery before fleeing in confusion; Union losses numbered around 200. Pemberton retreated back to Vicksburg, his army of 23,000 cut down to a third of its original size.

Vicksburg was now a city under siege. Pemberton wrote to Johnston, assuring him that he would hold out for as long as possible, but he knew that unless Johnston's army came to his relief, there was no chance of holding out for long. Johnston, however, did not come. If Jefferson Davis was similar to David Halleck, emphasizing the importance of places and positions over the outcomes of battles, Joseph E. Johnston was more like Grant. His own forces were not numerous enough to turn the tide at Vicksburg, and he wrote to Pemberton, saying that he was "too weak to save Vicksburg. Can do no more than attempt to save you and your garrison. It will be impossible to extricate you unless you co-operate." But by the time Johnston's offer of partial rescue reached Pemberton, the city was undergoing continuous shelling from the Union line. He could not venture out, and the 30,000 men Johnston had to offer him were overmatched by Grant's 80,000.

Finally, on July 3, 1863, with only a single day's rations remaining to his army, Pemberton sent word to Grant under a flag of truce. Just as Buckner had done at Ft. Donelson, Pemberton requested an armistice so that commissioners could meet to discuss terms of surrender. And again, as at Ft. Donelson, Grant replied that the only terms he would accept were immediate and unconditional surrender. "Men who have shown so much endurance and courage as those now in Vicksburg will always challenge the respect of an adversary, and I can assure you will always be treated with the respect due to prisoners of war," Grant informed Pemberton's aide de camp. But he agreed to meet face to face with Pemberton. Grant had little more to say than what he had already said, but he was willing to make one gesture towards the Confederates—not so much for their benefit, as because of the lessons he had learned after his victory at Ft. Donelson. On that occasion, Grant had discovered that it was extremely difficult for an army to take large numbers of prisoners without bogging itself down under a great deal of dead weight. The alternative was to allow the soldiers to go free on parole—they would sign oaths promising never to take up arms against the Union again, and then they would be free to go, surrendering their weapons but retaining their personal possessions. The officers would be permitted to keep their side arms. Pemberton was willing to agree to this, but he asked Grant to respect "the rights and property of citizens". In other words, he wanted Grant to let the Confederate officers keep their slaves. Grant denied this request, and Pemberton did not attempt to force the issue.

On July 4, 1863—the city of Vicksburg would not celebrate Independence Day again for another eighty years—Grant permitted 30,000 of Pemberton's men to go free on parole. The Union army now stood in complete control of the Mississippi River. The Confederacy was split in half, with the Union wedged squarely between the southeastern and southwestern states. In recognition of this achievement, Grant was promoted to major general, the highest rank that then existed in the regular army. He also received a personal letter from Abraham Lincoln:

"My Dear General:


"I do not remember that you and I ever met personally. I write this now as a grateful acknowledgment for the almost inestimable service you have done the country. I wish to say a word further. When you first reached the vicinity of Vicksburg, I thought you should do, what you finally did—march the troops across the neck, run the batteries with the transports, and thus go below; and I never had any faith, except a general hope that you knew better than I, that the Yazoo Pass expedition, and the like, could succeed. When you got below, and took Port Gibson, Grand Gulf, and vicinity, I thought you should go down the river and join Gen. Banks; and when you turned Northward East of the Big Black, I feared it was a mistake. I now wish to make the personal acknowledgment that you were right, and I was wrong."

# Chapter Five: Lieutenant General

## Lee at Gettysburg

For two months in the late summer of 1862, the Army of Northern Virginia, under the command of Robert E. Lee, had enjoyed a series of victories which drove the Union army under McClellan out of peninsular Virginia. Lee's attempt to force his way into the heart of Union territory had ended with his defeat at Antietam, but after defeating Ambrose Burnside at Fredericksburg and Joseph Hooker at Chancellorsville, he began to contemplate a second attempt, this time bypassing Washington and Baltimore and pushing farther north—into Pennsylvania. His chief objective was to gain control of the Baltimore & Ohio railroad, which connected Baltimore, the Union's largest port city, to the nation's capital. He had also hoped that his push north would draw the Union army away from Vicksburg, where Grant was still maneuvering around the Mississippi countryside, looking for a way to flank the city's defenses.

After Hooker's defeat at Chancellorsville, Lincoln placed Meade in control of the Army of the Potomac, with explicit instructions to follow Lee into Pennsylvania and halt his advance. When Lee got wind of Meade's pursuit, he began making arrangement for all Confederate forces in the area to regroup at the town of Gettysburg, but when the advanced guard arrived, it discovered that Meade's men had beaten them there. Miscommunication between Lee and one of his subordinates saved the Union forces from a rout. They retreated to a nearby area known as Cemetery Ridge, where they were joined by the rest of the Union army the next day. On July 2, full scale conflict ensued, resulting in nearly 9000 casualties on both the Union and Confederate sides.

On July 3, Lee ordered an offensive assault against the center of the Union line, over the protests of his second in command. Led by General George Pickett, a division of some 15,000 soldiers marched into the line of fire while the Union soldiers took aim from the shelter of stone battlements. Between half and three quarters of Pickett's men were killed; the advance would come to be known as "Pickett's Charge", and blame for the overwhelming losses sustained by his division would follow Pickett for the rest of his life. After the third day of fighting came to a close, Lee was forced to acknowledge that his second attempted northern invasion had no chance of success. The next day, July 4, Lee's forces retreated south to Virginia. The battle of Gettysburg and the siege of Vicksburg both ended in Confederate defeats on July 3, 1863.

Meade, like Halleck and McClelland and all the other Union generals save for Grant (and, increasingly, Sherman) avoided battle whenever possible. To Lincoln's immense frustration, Meade elected not to pursue Lee's retreating army. By the end of the fighting, Union casualties amounted to some 23,000 killed or wounded, with approximately 28,000 casualties on the Confederate side. Gettysburg was the bloodiest battle of the Civil War, but together with the fall of Vicksburg on July 3, it turned the tide of the conflict decisively in the Union's favor.

## Chattanooga

"Grant is my man," declared Lincoln after the fall of Vicksburg, "and I am his the rest of the war." It was a novelty for the president to have a general who took initiative and only communicated with the chain of command when strictly necessary. "He is a copious worker and a fighter," Lincoln observed to one of his aides,

"but a very meagre writer or telegrapher...
[Grant] doesn't worry and bother me. He isn't
shrieking for reinforcements all the time. He
takes what troops we can safely give him...and
does the best he can with what he has got." So
enamored with Grant was Lincoln that after
Meade allowed Lee's army to escape after
Gettysburg, he wanted to make Grant the
commander of the Army of the Potomac—the
army which commanded the entire eastern
theater of the war. But Grant expressed his wish
that he be allowed to remain with the armies of
the west, where he knew his men and his officers
and had an excellent grasp on the geography and
the terrain. Send him east, he explained, and he
would have to learn everything over from the
ground up.

Having declined this new command, Grant was
left with little to do for the rest of the summer of
1863. In September of that year, he was once
again injured when his horse, startled by the

shriek of a whistle, lost its footing and rolled on him. He suffered a crush injury to his knee that caused his entire leg and the right side of his body to grow painfully swollen. While he was in the hospital recovering, the Union armies suffered a severe setback in Tennessee. Confederate general Braxton Bragg staged a feigned retreat from the city of Chattanooga, luring Union general William Rosecrans, commanding the Army of the Cumberland, into seizing the seemingly abandoned city. If the Union could hold Chattanooga, it would command the road to Atlanta. However, unbeknownst to Rosecrans, Bragg had received heavy reinforcements, and quickly rounded on the Union army for a three day pitched battle that ended in heavy Union losses. It seemed that Chattanooga must fall back into Confederate hands, and soon.

Lincoln, observing that Rosecrans was as unsteady as "a duck that's been hit on the head", prompted Halleck to send Grant to Tennessee with reinforcements as soon as he was recovered enough to travel. Grant was not recovered, but he immediately traveled to Indianapolis to board a train for Louisville, where he had been told he would receive further instructions. As his train was pulling out of the station, it halted, and Edwin Stanton, Secretary of War, boarded. Taking a seat in Grant's compartment, Stanton produce two different versions of a presidential order. Both versions of the order began the same way: "By direction of the President of the United States, the Departments of the Ohio, of the Cumberland, and of the Tennessee, will constitute the Military Division of the Mississippi. Major General U.S. Grant, United States Army, is placed in command of the Military Division of the Mississippi, with his headquarters in the field." The second version of the order contained an additional paragraph which ordered William Rosecrans to be relieved of the command of the Army of the Cumberland, replaced by George Thomas. Stanton indicated to

Grant that it was up to him whether to keep Rosecrans or not. Grant elected to accept the second version of the order.

As soon as Grant arrived in Louisville and assumed command of the newly created Army of the Mississippi, he sent word to Rosecrans that he was relieved, and told his replacement, Thomas, to "hold Chattanooga at all hazards". Thomas replied that his army had only seven days' worth of rations left, but that they would "hold the town till we starve." Grant, who still needed crutches in order to walk, set out for Chattanooga instantly. Lincoln's order, establishing that the headquarters of the Army of the Mississippi were to be located "in the field", at once commanded Grant and gave him permission to do as he had always done when given the option, which was to go where the fighting was. The first order of business was to re-establish a supply line to Chattanooga, since Grant could not send for Sherman and Hooker's reinforcements unless he could feed them. Then, the general who had recently laid siege to Vicksburg had to figure out how to win the same battle in reverse, and break the Confederate siege against Chattanooga. A commander under siege is necessary on the defensive, but Grants entire modus operandi was to take the offensive position whenever possible. He was lucky in his officers; Thomas, selected by Grant to relieve Rosecrans from command, was cut very much from the same cloth as Grant, and his chief engineer, General William Smith, quickly won Grant's esteem by coming up with a prompt and intelligent plan to regain control of the Tennessee River, which would link Chattanooga with a Union supply depot located a few miles away. Within the week, the besieged soldiers were again eating full rations and receiving new clothes and weapons.

Thomas's staff was just as impressed with Grant as Grant was with them. One of them recorded this description of Grant as he appeared then:

"Many of us were not a little surprised to find him a man of slim figure, slightly stooped, five feet eight in height, weighing only 135 pounds. His eyes were dark-gray, and were the most expressive of his features. His hair and beard were of a chestnut brown color. The beard was worn full, no part of the face being shaved, but, like the hair, was always kept closely and neatly trimmed. His face was not perfectly symmetrical, the left eye being lower than the right. His voice was exceedingly musical, and one of the clearest in sound and most distinct in utterance that I have have ever heard. It had a singular power of penetration, and sentences spoken by him in an ordinary tone could be heard at a distance which was surprising. His gait of walking [was] decidedly unmilitary. He never carried his body erect, and having no ear for music or rhythm, he never kept step to the airs played by the bands, no matter how vigorously the bass drums emphasized the accent... When not pressed by any matter of importance he was often slow in his movements, but when roused to activity he was quick in every motion, and worked with marvelous rapidity. He was civil to all who came in contact with him, and never attempted to snub anyone, or treat anybody with less consideration on account of his inferiority in rank."

Bragg's Confederates were crawling over the mountains that ringed round Chattanooga. He had 70,000 men on the high ground; Thomas had about 45,000 in the town. It was one of the few occasions during the Civil War when the Confederates enjoyed such a pronounced numerical advantage. However, the Confederate leadership in Chattanooga was in turmoil. Braxton Bragg's staff officers had lost faith in him, and issued an appeal to President Jefferson

Davis to replace him. Davis, however, was particularly fond of Bragg, and disliked Joseph E. Johnston, his only viable replacement. Instead of dismissing Bragg, Davis reassigned all of Bragg's disgruntled staff officers. Then he ordered Grant's old friend, General James Longstreet, to leave Chattanooga and attack Union forces in Knoxville. As soon as Longstreet's divisions departed, Grant realized that the Confederates had surrendered their numerical advantage. He wanted to attack immediately, but George Thomas explained that so many of their horses had starved to death before the supply line was re-established that there was no way of transporting the heavy artillery to the proposed site of attack. Impatiently—it went against the grain of his soul for Grant not to take advantage of an exposed enemy weakness—he waited for Sherman to arrive with the men and horses they needed.

By the time Grant was ready to attack, it had begun to appear as though Bragg's forces were preparing to abandon the siege and slip away Atlanta. With no time to waste—Grant was receiving urgent telegrams from Washington, telling him to assist Burnside in Nashville—he ordered Thomas to attack Missionary Ridge, where the Confederates held a picket line. Thomas ordered his soldiers to go through the motions of a full dress parade, which captured the attention of the bored Confederate sentries. They were still watching with interest when Thomas abruptly ordered the guns turned around and opened fire on them. By the end of the day, Thomas had taken the ridge and extended the Union lines by a mile.

The assault on Missionary Ridge was a victory achieved against enormous odds. The Confederate position in the mountains was essentially unassailable, and the line was only broken due to the suicidal bravery of the Army of the Cumberland, which defied orders to charge up the mountain. (Curiously, the first regimental flag bearer to gain the top of Missionary Ridge was an eighteen-year old captain of the 24th Wisconsin named Arthur MacArthur—whose son Douglas would become one of the most famous generals of the second world war.) Grant attributed the Confederate defeat to the fact that Bragg had posted too many men across an easily defensible position—the men behind them, never expecting to fight unless they were ordered down the mountain, panicked in the face of the berserker Union charge. There was also the personal element to consider: when Bragg's staff officers lost faith in him, the mistrust quickly spread to the enlisted men. By contrast, Grant, Thomas, and Sherman worked in perfect harmony with each other, and Grant's men had unshakeable faith in him. They would do anything he asked, because they knew he always had a good reason for the decisions he made.

The Confederate soldiers who became Union prisoners of war after the battle of Chattanooga soon came to feel a certain measure of regard for Grant as well. One captured soldier later wrote that, after he and the other prisoners had been rounded up, a line of Union officers rode past them, none of them sparing a glance for the bedraggled southerners. Then: "When General Grant reached the line of ragged, filthy, bloody, despairing prisoners strung out on each side of the bridge, he lifted his hat and held it over his head until he passed the last man of that living funeral cortege. He was the only officer in that whole train who recognized us as being on the face of the earth."

## Lieutenant general

In March of 1864, Lincoln appointed Ulysses S. Grant lieutenant general and commander of all

Union armies, a rank held by no other general in U.S. military history since George Washington, who was given the rank after he took command of the American army after his second term as president. Assuming the rank of lieutenant general would automatically place Grant in a position of ultimate authority over everyone else in the army, including general in chief George Meade. He would be answerable to the President alone.

Since the beginning of his presidency, Lincoln had felt that it was necessary to take a direct hand in guiding the war because he, not having studied at West Point (or any other school, for that matter) had believed from the beginning that nothing short of the destruction of the rebel army could save the Union. Lincoln was an autodidact of the first water and knew more about warfare than most lawyers, but he often doubted the wisdom of his decisions as commander in chief because of his lack of formal military training. In Grant, Lincoln believed he had finally found the man who could be trusted to assume responsibility for the planning of the war. Lincoln told Grant that "He did not know but that [the military orders Lincoln had issued] were all wrong, and did know that some of them were. All he wanted or had ever wanted was someone who would take the responsibility and act, and call on him for all of the assistance needed, pledging himself to use all the power of the government in rendering such assistance." *Take the responsibility and act*—this was what Lincoln had been demanding of generals like Meade and Halleck for years, only to be repeatedly frustrated by their hesitancy. Grant had endeared himself to Lincoln because he was, if nothing else, a man of action.

But even as Congress debated the resolution that would confirm Grant's new rank, Lincoln hesitated over signing it. After Grant's victory at Chattanooga, a number of people had begun calling for Grant to run in the 1864 presidential election. Nowadays, the re-nomination of incumbent presidents is taken for granted, but this was not the case in the mid-19th century; with a few exceptions, it was an era of one-term presidencies. And the paucity of Union victories during the first two and a half years of the war had made Lincoln an unpopular president. If Grant were interested in taking Lincoln's place on the Republican ticket, Lincoln knew that he would have no dearth of supporters. And as much as he wanted to place Grant in command of the army, crowning him with the laurels last worn by George Washington would make it all the easier for Grant to supplant Lincoln politically.

To ease his mind, Lincoln reached out to one of Grant's oldest friends, J. Russell Jones of Illinois, and asked him point blank whether Grant had any interest in becoming president. As it happened, Grant had been deluged with mail from various members of both political parties on the subject of his running for office—and he had consigned all such letters to the wastebasket. Jones himself had written to Grant on the subject, advising him against a career in politics, and Grant had written back to say that, "I already have a pretty big job on my hands, and...nothing could induce me to think of being a presidential candidate, particularly so long as there is a possibility of having Mr. Lincoln re-elected." As it happened, Jones had received this letter from Grant the day before he was summoned to the White House, and he had it in his possession when he met with Lincoln. When Jones allowed Lincoln to read the letter, Lincoln's relief was palpable. "My son, you will never know how gratifying this is to me," he said. Lincoln signed off on Grant's promotion to lieutenant general and promptly invited Grant to Washington for their first face to face meeting.

Grant knew that the promotion was being debated in Congress, and he knew what accepting it would entail. But before heading east, he wrote to tell Sherman that he would probably refuse the position if it turned out that there was no way to do the job except from behind a desk in Washington. Yet, once Grant had arrived in the capital and conferred with Lincoln, Stanton, Meade, and others, he quickly saw that he *must* remain in Washington. He would not, however, remain behind a desk.

Grant's first priority, much to Lincoln's delight, was coordinating a massive military campaign that would simultaneously mobilize all the Union armies then in the field in a concerted effort to rout the Confederate forces under Lee, Johnston, Beauregard, Bragg, and others. Total war was required in order to bring the south to its knees once and for all. After attending a reception at the White House and presenting himself to Congress to formally accept his new rank, Grant visited the headquarters of the Army of the Potomac, where George Meade, who had been in some disgrace since allowing Lee's army to escape after Gettysburg, was patiently expecting to be relieved of his own command. Instead, Grant and Meade became fast friends after only a short conversation. Above all things, Grant prized unselfish honesty, and whatever his other failings, that was a quality Meade possessed. He told Grant that he would understand if Grant wished to replace him with one of the generals from the western theater, someone Grant knew and was accustomed to working with. According to Grant, Meade said that "the work before us was of such vast importance to the whole nation that the feeling or wishes of no one person should stand in the way of selecting the right men for all positions. For himself, he would serve to the best of his ability wherever placed." Grant came to believe that it was Halleck who was to blame for making Meade overly cautious, and that "with a more audacious general in chief" he would be able to do all that was needed.

Grant was already planning the so-called "march to the sea", the incursion by Union troops into the heartland of the south. He had intended to lead the march personally, but that would not be possible. Grant would not sit behind a desk, however; as before, his headquarters would be in the field, only this time with the Army of the Potomac, which Meade would continue to command. Sherman would assume Grant's old command over the Army of the Mississippi. Halleck would be appointed chief of staff and continue to work with Edwin Stanton, while taking his orders from Grant. Three days after arriving in Washington, Grant left again for Nashville to officially hand over command of the armies of the west to Sherman, and to confer with him and other senior officers from the western theater regarding what was to come. Grant's military secretary later wrote down his impressions of Grant and Sherman as they conferred over how best to end the war swiftly:

"Sherman was tall, angular and spare, as if his superabundant energy had consumed his flesh. His words were distinct, his ideas clear and rapid, coming, indeed, almost too fast for utterance, in dramatic, brilliant form. No one could be with him half an hour and doubt his greatness.

"Grant was calmer in manner a hundred fold. The habitual expression on his face was so quiet as to be almost incomprehensible. His manner, plain, placid, almost meek, in great moments disclosed to those who knew him well, immense, but still suppressed, intensity. In utterance he was slow and sometimes embarrassed, but the words were well-chosen, never leaving the remotest doubt of what he intended to convey.

"Not a sign about him suggested rank or reputation or power. He discussed the most ordinary themes with apparent interest, and turned from them in the same quiet tones, and without a shade of difference in his manner, to decisions that involved the fate of armies, as if great things and small were to him of equal moment. In battle, the sphinx awoke. The outward calm was even then not entirely broken; but the utterance was prompt, the ideas were rapid, the judgment was decisive, the words were those of command. The whole man became intense, as it were, with a white heat."

"The fate of armies" was weighing heavily on his mind—not only his own, but those of the Confederacy. His goal was to coordinate simultaneous offensives by all the Union armies so that Robert E. Lee and Joseph E. Johnston could not spare any of their own soldiers to reinforce the other man's army. Grant intended for this to be campaign that would end the war for good and all. The strategy, as Sherman later recalled, was simple: "He was to go for Lee and I was to go for Joe Johnston. That was the plan." Once Grant was certain that he and Sherman were on the same page, Grant returned to Washington.

Up to this point, only a few of the battles that had been fought so far were critical to the outcome of the war overall. The rest were, body counts notwithstanding, mere skirmishes in the larger scheme of things. The nineteen separate departments of the federal army had heretofore acted independently of one another, swatting at the Confederates when they moved into range but not moving towards any particular ultimate goal. Meanwhile, the distance between the different Union armies and the lack of concert in their movements enabled the Confederates to exploit the weaknesses in their over-extended communication lines and maneuver around them, or towards them, as they saw fit.

Dancing around the Union armies suited the Confederate generals. Lincoln and Grant wanted the war to end and the southern states to cease their rebellion—in other words, for the country to return to the antebellum status quo, inasmuch as that was possible. The Confederates had a different kind of goal in mind. Time was on their side. They merely needed to inflict enough Union casualties, and damage or seize enough Union territory, to make the war so unpopular in the north that Lincoln would be forced to offer some kind a peace settlement. Even if the south did not win independence—and by 1863, that was a very remote prospect—the Confederates were hopeful that Lincoln could be induced to offer peace terms that would permit them to keep their slaves. There were enough supporters of slavery still in the Union, and more importantly in Congress, to put Lincoln under considerable pressure to offer some kind of terms, unless the war could be brought to a swift end first. But Lincoln was determined to end the institution of slavery in the United States for all time, and he was depending on Grant to make the south buckle before his hand could be forced, or before he was voted out of office and replaced by a Northern democrat who would hasten to make peace with the Confederates. Grant's feelings about slavery were ambivalent—he once said that he had never been an abolitionist, or even what one would call "anti-slavery"—but he was obedient to the wishes of his president. And in the practical scheme of things, that was all that mattered.

"You and I, Mr. Stanton, have been trying to boss this job, and we have not succeeded very well with it," Lincoln informed his Secretary of War, once Stanton began to chafe under Grant's leadership. "We have sent across the mountains for Mr. Grant, as Mrs. Grant calls him, to relieve us, and I think we had better leave him alone to do as he pleases."

**The master plan**

Grant wasted no time in consolidating the scattered Union armies. All the armies positioned in the south—Florida, Georgia, and North and South Carolina—were sent to Virginia. Soldiers from the west were sent to New Orleans, ready to reinforce William Sherman as he began his march towards Atlanta. All Union soldiers then on furlough, officers and enlisted alike, were ordered to rejoin their commands. The plan, as Sherman said, was simple. The Army of the Potomac would engage Lee. "Wherever Lee goes," Grant told General Meade, "there you will go also." Sherman, commanding the Army of the Mississippi, was to "break...up [Johnston's army] and get into the interior of the enemy's country as far as you can, inflicting all the damage you can against their resources." Thanks to Grant's consolidation of Union forces, both Meade and Sherman were now commanding armies twice the size of their Confederate counterparts. Lee and Johnston would no longer be able to reinforce each other, but neither would they be able to draw enforcements from other far flung Confederate divisions. Even as Sherman prepared to advance into the deep south, Union soldiers were attacking Mobile, Alabama, in order to tie up Confederate reserve forces in the area. And while Meade began pursuing Lee, Union detachments would be cutting rail lines between Petersburg and the Confederate capital of Richmond, Virginia, while menacing Richmond itself from the south. Other Union divisions would advance on Richmond from the west and Lynchburg from the southwest, severing the Virginia & Tennessee rail lines.

Just before leaving Washington for field headquarters, Grant paid a final call on Lincoln, who warned him that he had a hard time keeping secrets, and therefore Grant shouldn't tell him too much about the fine details of his operations. As Grant later recalled, "He said he did not want to know my plans, for everybody he met was trying to find out from him something about the contemplated movements, and there was always a temptation to 'leak'." Grant therefore explained the plan in accurate, but reduced terms: he would use "the greatest number of troops practicable" and "employ all the force of all the armies continually and concurrently, so that there should be no recuperation on the part of the rebels, no rest from attack." The Union army could achieve much simply by advancing, even if they never engaged the enemy. Lincoln remarked, "Oh yes! I see that. As we say out West, if a man can't skin he must hold a leg while someone else does." At the beginning of the war, Lincoln had repeatedly suggested, to no avail, that the Union should "move at once upon the enemy's whole line so as to bring into action our great superiority in numbers". He was, accordingly, delighted with Grant's plans.

**Lee and Grant**

Since Grant was on the move with the Army of the Potomac in Virginia, and had perfect faith in Sherman's ability to command the west, he focused the main thrust of his energy on beating Lee, the best commander in the Confederate army. The Confederacy's hold on Virginia had been challenged by six different Union commanders already, and each of them had been soundly thrashed—Irvin McDowell at Manassas, McClellan on the peninsula, John Pope at Second Manassas, Burnside at Fredericksburg, Joe Hooker at Chancellorsville, and Meade at Mine Run. The string of Union defeats made Lee and his staff skeptical of Grant's ability to do anything except add his own name to the list of generals humiliated in Virginia. The only one of Lee's officers who understood the nature of what was coming for them was Grant's old friend, James Longstreet. "Do you know General Grant?" he asked his fellow officers. "Well, I do. I was with him for three years at West Point, I was present at his wedding, I served in the same army with him in Mexico, I have observed his methods of warfare in the West, and I believe I know him through and through. And I tell you we cannot afford to underrate him and the army he now commands. We must make up our minds to get into line of battle and stay there, for that man will fight us every day and every hour till the end of this war. In order to whip him we must outmaneuver him, and husband our strength as best we can."

In other words, Longstreet was proposing that Lee do as Grant was doing—look at the big picture, consolidate forces, and mobilize the full strength of the Confederate armies against Grant. But his warning went unheeded. What Longstreet may have recognized was that, quite apart from the personal qualities that made Grant so hazardous to his enemies in the field, he differed from the other six Union generals who had come to grief in Virginia in important ways.

Grant was now commanding one of the largest armies in history, and due to the nature of his rank as lieutenant general, he would not find himself bogged down by administrative interference from Washington. And he had trusted subordinates, like Sherman, to whom he could grant the same freedom and discretion that Lincoln had entrusted to him. He was also free to go where he pleased, along with his army, while Lee and all his command were more or less obliged to remain close to Richmond. Grant would not share the fate of his predecessors in Virginia.

At the same time, there was a reason why everyone who had faced Lee in Virginia had failed to injure him significantly. He was as different from other Confederate generals as Grant was from other Union generals, and it is possible he took Longstreet's warning not to underestimate Grant more seriously than his staff officers did. Lee had a network of scouts scattered throughout northern Virginia that supplied him with regular and reliable information about enemy movements. He also commanded the home turf advantage, quite literally; in order to strike at Lee, Union soldiers would have to proceed through "a desolate reach of pine barrens and scrub oak known as the Wilderness, a vast forbidding region, with few roads, and a dense undergrowth, making maneuver impossible and nullifying the Union's preponderance in men and artillery." It was "a doom-struck area familiar to every veteran of the Army of the Potomac."

Lee's ability to predict Grant's movements was not perfect, but it was far superior to that of any other Confederate commander Grant had faced. At first, Lee was convinced that Grant meant to attack Richmond at his earliest opportunity. It was what any West Pointer who subscribed to the places theory of war would have done. Capturing the Confederate capital, which was also the south's most important rail hub, would strike a devastating blow against Confederate morale. Since Grant was as much responsible for protecting Washington as Lee was for protecting Richmond, Lee had good reason to assume that Grant would prioritize a strike against the city. In reality, Grant was only heading in a Richmond-like direction because he knew that Lee was defending it; Lee and his army, not the city itself, was his object. Halleck had been satisfied to take possession of Corinth after it had been deserted by Beauregard, but Grant had little interest in taking possession of a deserted Richmond, whatever the symbolic value of such a coup. If he arrived in Richmond, he wanted Lee's army to be there, so he could destroy it.

In other ways, however, Lee did possess something that one historian refers to as a "schooled insight bordering on clairvoyance" when it came to predicting Grant's movements. As soon as the Army of the Potomac mobilized,

Lee informed Jefferson Davis that Grant would launch three simultaneous, separate attacks against the Confederate army, one from the front, one from the east, and one in the Shenandoah valley. Lee spent two months studying Grant's movements, analyzing the situation as he would do were he in Grant's shoes. He anticipated a few locations where Grant's army might ford the Rapidan river, but he decided not to meet Grant in combat there. Instead, he would pull back into "the Wilderness," then attack with his full strength, until Grant, like all his predecessors, had no choice but to beat a hasty retreat. When Grant saw that Lee was nowhere to be found as his army crossed the Rapidan, he would think that he had taken Lee by surprise, little knowing that Lee was biding his time, waiting for Grant to come to him.

# Chapter Six: The Sphinx Awakens

## The Overland Campaign

From May 5 to June 24, 1864, Grant's army clashed with Lee's in fourteen distinct battles and skirmishes in what became known as the Overland Campaign. The Battle of the Wilderness took place across the first two days of fighting, May 5 to May 7. Grant anticipated that Lee's forces would leave their entrenchments after the Union army crossed the Rapidan on May 4, but because he believed his arrival had taken Lee by surprise he was unprepared for the rapidity of Lee's response. Meade's plan, approved by Grant, was for the Army of the Potomac to advance through the Wilderness at a forced march, which would enable it to get clear of the treacherous terrain in less than a day. Once they realized that Lee was on the move, however, it became apparent that they would not be able to maneuver quickly enough to reach open ground before the fighting started. The men could get through the trees in a day, but their wagon convoy could not—and here on the statewide battleground that was northern Virginia, it was impossible to abandon their supplies and live off the land, as Grant's men had done back west. Grant made the decision to slow the march of the infantry so that they could keep pace with and protect the wagon train. It would mean spending more time in the Wilderness, but they still did not anticipate fighting there—they still had not realized how quickly Lee was closing in on them.

Much like Grant, Lee had a simple objective: trap the Army of the Potomac in the Wilderness, destroy them, and effectively end the war in a single battle. Lee had only eight divisions under his command, compared to Grant's fifteen, but he was trusting in the Wilderness to equalize the odds. At 6 a.m. on the morning of May 5, the commander of Meade's 5th Corps spotted Lee's army "ready and waiting in line of battle". It would shortly be Lee's turn to be surprised, however. Rather than retreating and joining the main body of the army, Meade's men carried out the order which Grant had given him: "If any opportunity presents itself for pitching into a part of Lee's army, do so without giving time for disposition."

The Wilderness shielded and sheltered Lee's soldiers, and it disoriented Grant's, just as Lee expected. But after two days of fighting, the Confederate and Union armies were at a draw. The two-day battle had encompassed "the most ferocious fighting yet seen in North America". Union casualties were around 18,000 men lost, missing, or wounded; Confederate losses came to about 11,000. Both generals had suffered the loss of 18% of their armies. These were the sorts of losses that had persuaded Joe Hooker to abandon the Wilderness after Chancellorsville, but Grant had no intention of retreating. He was optimistic despite the heavy losses, because "we remain in possession of the field" while "the Confederates have withdrawn into a defensive position. We cannot call the engagement a positive victory, but the enemy have only twice actually reached our lines in their many attacks, and on both occasions they were repulsed." Grant announced that the army would leave the Wilderness and advance towards Richmond. Lee would then have no choice but to interpose his army between Grant and the Confederate capital.

Lee had also realized that there was no point remaining in the Wilderness, even though it had protected him in the past. The Confederate army could not resupply its losses, as Grant's army could. He needed to withdraw to a more secure location and build entrenchments, so that the next time the Union army struck they would be attacking a fortified position. And he knew that Grant, unlike every other Union general he had faced in those woods, would follow wherever he went. Spotsylvania Court House lay twelve miles down the road that led towards Richmond. Both Grant and Lee were in a race to reach the court house first, but Grant, still unaccustomed to how things worked in the Army of the Potomac, could not get his divisions up and moving as quickly as he wanted, and by the time he reached Spotsylvania, Lee was there waiting for him. The Civil War saw rapid advancements in the use of trench warfare and Lee in particular had a knack for building wood-and-earth entrenchments that, in one Union officer's estimation, effectively multiplied his defensive strength by a factor of four. Lee's army was in a desperate condition, far more so than even Grant realized, but this did not prevent the Confederates from holding Spotsylvania for two weeks, from May 8 to May 21.

Just as in the Wilderness, Grant eventually withdrew and set back down the road to Richmond. He fought Lee at Yellow Tavern on

May 11; at Meadow Bridge on May 12; at North Anna and Wilson's Wharf from May 23 to May 26; across the Pamunkey River from May 27 to May 29; at Cold Harbor, where Grant's army sustained 6000 casualties, from May 31 to June 12; across the James River from June 12 to June 18; and at St. Mary's Church on June 24. But once Grant had crossed the James River, Lee understood that the worst had come to pass for the Confederacy. The James provided access to the Appomattox River, where lay the city of Petersburg. Located just south of Richmond, the Confederate capital was heavily dependent on Petersburg, which contained major supply depots and the most important rail hub in the south. If Petersburg fell into Union hands, the fall of Richmond was virtually guaranteed.


The Overland Campaign resulted in devastating loss of human life. Grant's army suffered some 55,000 casualties in total, amounting to about 45% of his entire army, while the Army of

Northern Virginia suffered 33,600 casualties, amounting to 50% of Lee's forces. But Grant had achieved what no other Union commander had managed to achieved—he had engaged Lee where he was strongest and forced him into a corner. The campaign had taken its toll on Grant personally, particularly after the battle of Cold Harbor, which was the most serious tactical defeat Grant suffered throughout the entire war, but the same quiet, understated faith which had sustained him and his soldiers at Shiloh and Chattanooga was at his service after Cold Harbor. Colonel Adam Badeau of the Army of the Potomac later wrote that,

"Neither the skill of his opponent, nor the splendid fighting of the rebel army; neither the disappointment when he saw his immediate plans frustrated; nor his chagrin when his troops found the hostile works impregnable; neither the unavoidable losses which his army sustained, and which no man appreciated more acutely or deplored more profoundly than he; neither the increasing responsibilities nor the settling gloom of this terrible and seemingly endless campaign—depressed or discourage, so far as those nearest him could discover, this imperturbably man. He believed, all through these anxious days and weary nights, that if he had not accomplished a positive victory, he was yet advancing, not only toward Richmond, but toward the goal he had proposed to himself, the destruction of Lee and of the rebellion."

## Appomattox

"We must destroy this army of Grant's before it gets to the James River," Robert E. Lee remarked to Jubal Early, during the battle of Cold Harbor. "If he gets there it will become a siege, and then it will be a mere question of time." Lee's assessment proved correct. The siege of

Petersburg lasted for nearly ten months—from June 9, 1864, to March 25, 1865. It was not a siege in the same sense that the assault on Vicksburg had been a siege. Petersburg was not built on a bluff, or defended by moat-like swamps. It began with a frontal assault by Grant against Petersburg, after which the Union soldiers built their entrenchments and settled in for a long onslaught.

The Army of Northern Virginia was fighting a losing battle from the beginning. If it had not been for the determination of the Confederate soldiers and their faith in Lee, which was as profound as the faith that the Union soldiers had in Grant, the war would have been over sooner. But Lee was sustained in part by the hope that the upcoming presidential elections would oust Abraham Lincoln from office. The Democratic presidential candidate, former Union general George McClellan, was running on an anti-war platform. In the summer and early fall of 1864,

Lincoln's popularity was at an all time low. Though Grant and Lincoln both were convinced that the Union would be victorious if Grant held to his present course, they were both in an agony of doubt that he would be permitted to do so. The average American voter saw only that Grant's army had been sitting seemingly idly outside Petersburg for months and that Sherman had yet to take Atlanta.

The so-called "Crater fiasco" at Petersburg further eroded public confidence in Lincoln and his favorite general. In August, Grant had paid a visit to Washington to confer with Sheridan about his campaign in the Shenandoah valley, where he was waiting to head Lee off in the event that his army managed to do what Grant had done at Cold Harbor—that is, sneak away from the battle by marching one division after another parallel to the front line of battle, the final divisions stealing away in the night, so that the Confederates simply woke up one morning and found that the enemy had vanished. That Lee might attempt such an escape was Grant's greatest fear; given the fact that the Army of Northern Virginia had been reduced to a fraction of its original size, Lee would be able to accomplish the maneuver all the more easily. But Stanton and others in the War Department were questioning the wisdom of Sheridan's positioning himself south of the Confederate army, so Grant felt it necessary to see Sheridan in person and make it clear to him that Sheridan answered only to him and that he was authorized to ignore any grumbling he might hear.

While Grant was away from Petersburg, however, a carefully planned Union operation fell to pieces. Soldiers and engineers under Burnside's command had tunneled 511 feet under the Confederate earthworks and stocked the tunnel with four tons of gunpowder, with the intention of "blowing the rebel line to Kingdom Come". After the gunpowder was ignited, two

Unions corps were supposed to charge through the gap and tear a hole through the Confederate army. Burnside had created a new division, composed entirely of free black soldiers, to handle the detonation and lead the charge through. The black soldiers had been specially trained for this mission, but at the last moment, Meade ordered Burnside to have a white division lead the assault. The white division commander was a notorious drunkard and was intoxicated when the munitions were detonated. The resulting explosion certainly managed to destroy the Confederate works, but it also created a crater 170 feet long and thirty feet deep. An entire Confederate regiment was buried beneath it, but the follow-up charge by Union soldiers was disorderly and failed to exploit the advantage. Most humiliatingly of all, Union soldiers had to climb down into the crater and then up the other side in order to reach the Confederates. Most of them slid right back down into the crater again, which made them such easy pickings for the Confederates on the high ground that one of the soldiers then present described it as a "turkey shoot". Grant was deeply disheartened—properly executed, the explosion should have wiped out a large chunk of Lee's army. But he was even more fearful that the debacle would hurt Lincoln's chances of re-election.

"The rebels are down to their last man," Grant wrote to his old patron, Elihu Washburne. "A man lost by them cannot be replaced. They have robbed the cradle and the grave equally to get their present force. Besides what they lose in frequent skirmishes and battles they are now losing from desertions and other causes at least one regiment a day. With this drain upon them the end is visible if we will be true to ourselves." Grant told Washburne that Lee was trying to bide time until after the election. "They hope for a counter revolution. They hope for the election of the peace candidate." To an old childhood friend, Commodore Daniel Ammen, Grant expressed his fear for what would happen if a "peace candidate" should be elected. "It would be but the beginning of the war," he said. "The demands of the South would know no limits. They would demand indemnity for expenses incurred in carrying on the war. They would demand return of all their slaves...and they would keep on demanding until it would be better dead than submit longer."

As it turned out, Lincoln's political fortunes were about to turn on a dime. On September 2, 1864 the War Department received a telegram reading, simply: "GENERAL SHERMAN HAS TAKEN ATLANTA".

## Sherman's Atlanta campaign and march to the sea

Atlanta, Georgia, was one of the most important rail and manufacturing centers in Confederate territory, and Sherman had been cutting a swathe down the center of the Confederate heartland to reach it for months. Joseph E. Johnston's forces were encamped in Dalton, Georgia, not far from Atlanta, but Johnston refused to make any offensive moves again Sherman—rather, he waited while slowly amassing reinforcements in an attempt to balance out the numerical odds, which were stacked against him.

In Virginia, Grant's 2 to 1 numerical superiority enabled him to pursue battle heatedly, since he could replace his casualties, while Lee could not. But Sherman took a cagier approach, choosing not to make a direct assault against Johnston's forces with his full strength. Instead, two of Sherman's divisions engaged Johnston in a diversionary battle, while a third division crept around the Confederate flank to attack the railroad line that was supplying Johnston with reinforcements. Between May and June, Sherman's forces attacked so many times that Johnston's army was forced to retreat and regroup in Atlanta.

Around this point, Jefferson Davis replaced Johnston with General John Hood, who Davis perceived as being more aggressive and less likely to cede ground without a fight. Hood directed two offensive attacks against Sherman's men, the second of which, at Peachtree Creek just outside Atlanta, was nearly successful. The city of Atlanta was surrounded by formidable fortifications; rather than assault them directly, Sherman concentrated his efforts on a push westward, where the sole remaining railroad line coming into Atlanta lay. Hood's men defended the railroad through all of July and August, and eventually Sherman began to bombard the city with artillery. On August 25, Sherman's men were successful in cutting the railroad line, and

Hood's men were forced to evacuate Atlanta within a week, on September 1. Sherman took control of the city on September 2.

After fleeing Atlanta, Hood would split his army into two commands, both marching west, to Alabama and Tennessee respectively. Sherman sent 60,000 of his troops, under the command of George Thomas, to engage the Confederate Army of Tennessee at Nashville. The other 62,0000, Sherman led personally in an advance towards Savannah, in what has come to be known as Sherman's March to the Sea.

Years before, in Missouri, Grant had discovered that he could afford to separate his army from its own supply lines because his soldiers were capable of living off the land. Later, after Shiloh, Grant realized that if his army could live off the land, so could the Confederates—and therefore, if he was to bring the southern armies to their knees, he would have to deprive them of the ability to seize food, water, livestock, horses, shelter, or anything else that would make their lives easier. In the early days of the war, as his proclamation to the citizens of Paducah demonstrates, Grant had preferred to leave private proper in private hands and inflict as little hardship on civilians as possible, so long as they were not actively working against Union interests. After Shiloh, he reversed that policy. Southern civilians were not to be harmed, but all property that could conceivably be of use to the Confederate army would be seized. Even if, like a captured soldier released on parole, they promised not to give aid or comfort to Confederate soldiers, there was nothing to stop desperate, hungry soldiers from taking them by force. The only way to deprive them of such resources was to confiscate them or destroy them.

It was for this reason that Sherman's armies destroyed farms and factories, burned houses, and generally wreaked as much destruction as humanly possible during the march south. They stole as much food as they could carry and burned everything they could not use, killing livestock and burning crops. Sherman, to this day, has a popular reputation for savagery due to these "total war" tactics; scarcely any of his detractors seem to take much notice of the fact that he was acting on Grant's orders. After battles with heavy Union casualties, Grant was occasionally vilified as a butcher by northern newspapers, but that reputation has not pursued him over the past 132 years the way that Sherman's has.

Both Grant and Sherman espoused these scorched earth policies for a simple reason: in the long run, they believed, it was the more merciful option. Sherman wrote, "You cannot qualify war in harsher terms than I will. War is cruelty, and you cannot refine it; and those who brought war into our country deserve all the curses and maledictions a people can pour out. I know I had no hand in making this war, and I know I will make more sacrifices to-day than any of you to secure peace." The only merciful war was a short war, in other words. Whatever else may be said or understood about Sherman's march to the sea, it achieved the stated objective of making it impossible for the fighting to continue. The destructive power of Sherman's army was so great that Hood's army eventually gave up trying to fight them, instead charging ahead to destroy their own bridges and roads, in an attempt to slow the Union army's progress. When Sherman reached Savannah on December 21, 1864, he was expecting to find ten thousand Confederate soldiers ready to defend the city; instead, they found that Savannah had been abandoned to its fate.

## Appomattox

Sherman's victory, preceding the fall of Petersburg by six months, saved the Union from collapse by saving Lincoln's presidency. Lincoln was so certain that the country would remain divided forever if he was voted out of office that he had written a memorandum, only a week before the fall of Atlanta, which read:

"This morning, as for some days past, it seems exceedingly probably that this Administration will not be reelected. Then it will be my duty to cooperate with the President-elect as to save the Union between the election and the inauguration; as he will have secured his election on such ground that he cannot possibly save it afterwards."

He then presented the memorandum to his cabinet, with the blank back side of the page facing up, and demanded that they all sign it without reading it.

At the same time, Lee was attempting to explain to his own president's administration that his army was in grave danger of being captured or defeated. "Unless some measure can be devised to replace our losses, the consequences may be disastrous," he warned Confederate Secretary of War James Seddon. "[Without reinforcements] I cannot see how we are to escape the natural military consequences of the enemy's numerical superiority."

By October, the Confederate line at Petersburg stretched for thirty-five miles, making it disastrously vulnerable to attack. Further south, John Hood's Army of the Tennessee was pursuing Sherman's Army of the Mississippi in an attempt to wreak vengeance for Atlanta. Jefferson Davis announced that Sherman's forces would soon meet with "the fate that befell the army of the French Empire in its retreat from Moscow". When this remark was conveyed to Grant, he seemed to find it humorous. "Who is to furnish the snow?" he inquired dryly. In December of 1864, General George Thomas, whose men had led the Missionary Ridge charge at Shiloh, met the Army of the Tennessee in battle and effectively destroyed it. There was now nothing left of the Confederacy, save for South Carolina, North Carolina, and the southernmost part of Virginia. The value of Confederate currency plummeted until it was scarcely worth the paper it was printed on. Richmond began starving, as Sheridan destroyed the crops that were supplying it from the Shenandoah valley. An estimated 8% of the Army of Northern Virginia deserted every month, carrying off still more Confederate soldiers that Lee could not afford to lose. The end was near, and Lee knew it.

His last hope for his starving, beleaguered army after 293 days of siege was to abandon the defense of Richmond and Petersburg. On April 2, 1865, Lee told Jefferson Davis, "I see no prospect of doing more than holding our position here till night. I am not certain that I can do that. If I can I shall withdraw tonight north of the Appomattox...I advise that all preparations be made for leaving Richmond tonight." The Confederate government in Richmond promptly moved to Danville, Virginia, near the border with North Carolina. Lee's hope was to march southwest to North Carolina himself, where he would combine his army with that of Joseph E. Johnston. He hoped to reach the Richmond & Danville Railroad; there were four freight trains filled with food rations headed his way, and the rail line was the last link between southern Virginia and North Carolina. Sheridan, however, reached the trains first and cut the rail line. There was no escape route left, no supplies coming, and no hope whatsoever for what little remained of the Army of Northern Virginia—unless Lee surrendered.

Grant received a dispatch from Brigadier General Philip Sheridan on April 7, 1865, indicating that he was planning to strike from the south and cut off Lee's retreat by seizing the railroad (and the food trains). Grant read the message quietly to himself, growing very quiet. Then, suddenly, he announced to his staff: "I have a great mind to summon Lee to surrender." He then took out his dispatch book and wrote the following letter:

"The results of the last week must convince you of the hopelessness of further resistance on the part of the Army of Northern Virginia in this struggle. I feel that it is so, and regard it as my duty to shift from myself the responsibility of any further effusion of blood by asking of you the surrender of that portion of the Confederate States army known as the Army of Northern Virginia."

Lee's reply arrived later that same night: "I have received your note of this date. Though not entertaining the opinion you express of the hopelessness of further resistance on the part of the Army of N. Va.—reciprocate your desire to avoid the useless effusion of blood, and therefore before considering your proposition, ask the terms you will offer on condition of its surrender."

Grant replied first thing the next morning: "Peace being my great desire, there is but one condition I would insist upon—namely, the men and officers surrendered shall be disqualified for taking up arms against the Government of the United States until properly exchanged [*ed. Exchanged for captured Union officers of equivalent rank*]. I will meet you, or will designate officers to meet any officers you may name for the same purpose, at any point agreeable to you, for the purpose of arranging definitely the terms upon which the surrender of the Army of Northern Virginia will be received."

Lee's next reply was equivocal. He did not yet know, though Grant did, that Sheridan had beaten him to Appomattox and seized the railway. He wrote to Lee again, and after the exchange of several more short messages, Lee requested a face to face meeting. Grant later recorded in his memoirs that he was suffering from a bad migraine when he received Lee's note, but that it vanished as soon as he read its contents.

On April 9, 1865, Lee, accompanied only by his secretary and a single orderly who carried the flag of truce—a dirty handkerchief tied to a stick—set out to meet Grant. He was in an agony of uncertainty regarding the surrender terms that "Unconditional Surrender" Grant might demand of him, especially now that Lee was no longer in a position to offer him any realistic threat of refusal. His men were sick, ragged, and starving to death, and probably would not survive long as prisoners of war. James Longstreet had assured him that Grant would offer the same terms to him that Lee would offer to Grant if their positions were reversed; but it was not until Grant actually committed those terms to paper that Lee allowed himself to feel any relief.

Grant had offered Lee his choice of meeting places, and Lee's scout had located a house in Appomattox belonging to one Wilmer McLean, who was willing to allow them to use it for the purposes of the meeting. Lee presented himself for the interview attired in a clean new gray uniform, wearing a red silk sash around his waist, and carrying a ceremonial sword with an ornate hilt at his side. It was not his customary dress uniform; he had made a special effort with his appearance because he thought that he might shortly become Grant's prisoner, and he hoped to cut as impressive a figure as possible, for the sake of the south. Grant, who arrived after Lee, was by contrast attired in his customary battlefield garb—a flannel shirt, dirty trousers, muddy boots, and nothing to indicate his rank except for his epaulets. A member of his own staff remarked that, compared to Lee, "Grant, covered with mud in an old faded uniform, looked like a fly on a shoulder of beef."

Grant and Lee took seats by the fire and began to chat, at first on general subjects. Grant reminded Lee that they had met once before, during the Mexican-American War. Lee replied that he recalled the meeting, and had often tried since then to remember what Grant looked like. "What General Lee's feelings were I do not know,"

Grant later wrote. "As he was a man of much dignity, with an impassive face, it was impossible to say whether he felt inwardly glad that the end had finally come, or felt sad over the result, and was too manly to show it. Whatever his feelings, they were entirely concealed from my observation; but my own feelings, which had been quite jubilant on the receipt of his letter, were sad and depressed. I felt like anything rather than rejoicing at the downfall of a foe who had fought so long and valiantly."

Presently, Lee came to the point. "I suppose, General Grant, that the object of our present meeting is fully understood. I asked to see you to ascertain upon what terms you would receive the surrender of my army." Grant explained his terms—and then, in Lee's presence, he carried his battered dispatch book to the desk and set them down in writing:

"In accordance with the substance of my letter to you of the 8th inst., I propose to receive the surrender of the Army of N. Va. on the following terms, to wit: Rolls of all the officers and men to be made in duplicate. One copy to be given to an officer designated by me, the other to be retained by such officer or officers as you may designate. The officers to give their individual paroles not to take up arms against the Government of the United States until properly exchanged, and each company or regimental commander sign a like parole for the men of their commands. The arms, artillery and public property to be parked and stacked, and turned over to the officer appointed by me to receive them. This will not embrace the side-arms of the officers, nor their private horses or baggage. This done, each officer and man will be allowed to return to their homes, not to be disturbed by United States authority so long as they observe their paroles and the laws in force where they may reside."

This was more generosity than Lee had expected; in fact, strictly speaking, it was more generosity than Grant was authorized to give. But Grant answered to no one but Lincoln, and when it came to the fate of the defeated Confederate army, Lincoln and Grant had already established that they were on the same page. Grant would technically have been within his rights to arrest Lee and all his officers and take his army captive. Instead, he effectively pardoned the entire Army of Northern Virginia for the crime of treason. During a visit to Washington the previous March, Grant had met with Sherman and Lincoln. Sherman had asked the president, "What is to be done with the rebel armies when defeated?" Lincoln spoke at some length of his desire to offer the Confederates the most generous terms possible. He wanted to "get the men comprising the Confederate armies back to their homes, at work on their farms, and in their shops." Lincoln was confident that "they won't take up arms again. Let them go, officers and all. I want submission and no more bloodshed... I want no one punished; treat them liberally all round. We want those people to return to their allegiance to the Union and submit to the laws." Even Jefferson Davis and his cabinet were to be spared; or at least, that was the meaning that Grant took from Lincoln's "telling the story of a teetotaler who was asked if he wanted his lemonade spiked with whiskey. The man replied that if he didn't know it, he supposed it would be all right." In other words, if Jefferson Davis and the rest were to quietly slip out of the country, Lincoln would lose no sleep over it. (As it happens, Davis briefly contemplated going into exile in Cuba, but instead remained in the country. He was arrested and imprisoned on the orders of Andrew Johnson after the assassination of Abraham Lincoln, but was released after two years without a trial.)

Lee expressed his acceptance of the terms that Grant was offering. His only request was that the Confederate cavalrymen and artillery soldiers, like the officers, be allowed to keep their horses—unlike their Union counterparts, they had brought their horses with them from home when they enlisted. Grant was surprised. "I did not know that any private soldiers owned their own animals, but I think this will be the last battle of the war—I sincerely hope so—and I take it that most of the men in the ranks are small farmers, and as the country has been so raided by the two armies, it is doubtful whether they will be able to put in a crop to carry themselves and their families through the next winter without the aid of the horses they are now riding. I will arrange it this way: I will not change the terms as now written, but I will instruct the officers I shall appoint to receive the paroles to let all the men who claim to own a horse or a mule to take the animals home with them to work their little farms."

Lee was grateful; he was even more grateful when Grant offered to give his starving men

25,000 food rations. By four in the afternoon of April 9, it was done. When Lee rode away, the Union soldiers began to cheer, but Grant ordered them to stop. Now that Lee's army had surrendered, his soldiers were once again to be regarded as fellow citizens, and it was unseemly to rejoice in a countryman's downfall. A formal ceremony of surrender followed the next day. The Confederate soldiers filed in, stacked their weapons under the watchful eye of Major General Joshua L. Chamberlain and two brigades of Union soldiers that were lined up facing one another. Historian Jean Edward Smith describes the scene that followed:

"As [Lieutenant General John B. Gordon] approached, Chamberlain gave a brief order and a bugle sounded. Instantly the Union line from right to left, regiment by regiment in succession, shifted from order arms to carry arms, the marching salute. Hearing the familiar snap and rattle of the muskets, Gordon looked up in surprise, caught the meaning, and wheeled to face Chamberlain, 'making himself and his horse one uplifted figure, with profound salutation as he dropped the point of his sword to his boot toe.' Gordon then turned and ordered each Confederate brigade to march past the Union troops at carry arms, honor answering honor, a soldier's mutual salutation and farewell. In perfect order, the men stacked arms and cartridge boxes and laid down their flags. General Gordon, his eyes moist, addressed the men from horseback, urging them to depart in peace, to obey the laws and work for the future of the united nation."

Grant telegraphed news of Lee's surrender to Edwin Stanton: "General Lee surrendered the Army of Northern Virginia this afternoon on terms proposed by myself. The accompanying additional correspondence will show the conditions fully."

# Reconstruction

After news of Lee's surrender traveled south, the remaining Confederate forces lost heart for further fighting. Just over a week after Lee's surrender, on April 18, 1865, Joseph E. Johnston surrendered to William Sherman in Durham, North Carolina. Grant, meanwhile, traveled to Washington to "begin the process of winding down the war". He ordered the Quartermaster General to halt the purchase of any additional supplies, discharge all wounded soldiers, and put an end to the draft. Grant then accompanied Lincoln on a three-day whirlwind tour of Washington, exhibiting himself to the admiring crowds.

On April 14, 1865, Lincoln invited Grant and his wife Julia to accompany a party consisting of himself, Mrs. Lincoln, and two others, to see a performance of *Our American Cousin* at Ford's Theater. Grant declined because "some incident of a trifling nature had made [Julia] resolve to leave [Washington]that day." In truth, Julia Grant had refused the Lincolns' invitation because she could not abide Mary Todd Lincoln and had no wish to spend an evening in her company. That evening they boarded a train bound for Philadelphia. When they reached their hotel, a telegram from the War Department was waiting for Grant. He read it in stunned silence before handing it to Julia:

"THE PRESIDENT WAS ASSASSINATED AT FORD'S THEATER AT 10:30 TONIGHT AND CANNOT LIVE. THE WOUND WAS A PISTOL SHOT THROUGH THE HEAD. SECRETARY SEWARD AND HIS SON FREDERICK WERE ALSO ASSASSINATED AT THEIR RESIDENCE AND ARE IN A DANGEROUS CONDITION. THE SECRETARY OF WAR DESIRES THAT

YOU RETURN TO WASHINGTON
IMMEDIATELY."

Unbeknownst to Grant, he, like Lincoln and
Seward, had also been a target in John Wilkes
Booth's assassination plot. Expecting to find
Grant and his wife in the theater box with
Lincoln, Booth had planned to stab Grant before
shooting the president. During a brief stop in
Maryland on the way to Philadelphia, someone
had attempted to force entry onto Grant's train
car, only to be rebuffed by the conductor. The
following day, as Julia Grant would record in her
memoirs, the Grants received a letter which
read: "General Grant, thank God, as I do, that
you still live. It was your life that fell to my lot,
and I followed you on the train. Your car door
was locked and thus you escaped me, thank
God."

For the rest of his life, Grant would bitterly regret the fact that he had not attended the theater with the Lincolns that night. He was convinced that, had he been present, he would have heard Booth entering the theater box, and could have protected Lincoln. The day that Abe Lincoln died was "the darkest day of my life," Grant later told a journalist. "I did not know what it meant. Here was the Rebellion put down in the field, and starting up in the gutters. We had fought it as war, now we had to fight it as assassination."

Lincoln's assassination was not the beginning of a new war, but it was the beginning of a new stage in Grant's life and career. Greatly concerned that Andrew Johnson, Lincoln's vice president and successor, was vindictive against the south, where Lincoln had been forgiving and liberal, Grant would run against Johnson in the presidential election of 1868. He would not only win the presidency, but he would be the last president elected to two successive terms in office until Woodrow Wilson's re-election in 1916.

For many decades after Grant's death, his presidency was underrated by historians, who consistently ranked him as being among the least effective chief executives in American history. But this is due largely to the fact that Grant was dedicated to the Reconstruction effort, and to preserving the rights of newly free black Americans across the country. When Lincoln was president, there had been a great deal of discussion as to how black Americans could be integrated into white society, but after the assassination, and certainly by the time Grant was elected, the public had grown tired of the debate. They no longer cared that a de facto state of slavery still existed in many parts of the south. But Grant's second inaugural address makes it clear that the welfare of former slaves, as well as

Native Americans, was at the forefront of his mind:

"The theory of government changes with general progress. Now that the telegraph is made available for communicating thought, together with rapid transit by steam, all parts of a continent are made contiguous for all purposes of government, and communication between the extreme limits of the country made easier than it was throughout the old thirteen States at the beginning of our national existence.

"The effects of the late civil strife have been to free the slave and make him a citizen. Yet he is not possessed of the civil rights which citizenship should carry with it. This is wrong, and should be corrected. To this correction I stand committed, so far as Executive influence can avail.

"Social equality is not a subject to be legislated upon, nor shall I ask that anything be done to advance the social status of the colored man, except to give him a fair chance to develop what there is good in him, give him access to the schools, and when he travels let him feel assured that his conduct will regulate the treatment and fare he will receive...

"My efforts in the future will be directed to the restoration of good feeling between the different sections of our common country... and, by a humane course, to bring the aborigines of the country under the benign influences of education and civilization. It is either this or war of extermination: Wars of extermination, engaged in by people pursuing commerce and all industrial pursuits, are expensive even against the weakest people, and are demoralizing and wicked. Our superiority of strength and advantages of civilization should make us lenient toward the Indian. The wrong inflicted upon him should be taken into account and the balance placed to his credit. The moral view of the question should be considered and the question asked, Can not the Indian be made a useful and productive member of society by proper teaching and treatment? If the effort is made in good faith, we will stand better before the civilized nations of the earth and in our own consciences for having made it."

As a military commander, Grant's influence on modern warfare is unrivaled. One biographer estimates that "his systematic deployment of overwhelming force...established the strategic doctrine that became the basis for American triumphs in two world wars and...in the Persian Gulf." The boy who had never wanted to be a soldier in the first place made his mark as one of the greatest soldiers in American history, his accomplishments unequaled by anyone, save perhaps George Washington.

Grant did not want to be president any more than he had wanted to attend West Point, but he chose to pursue politics in order to insure that the peace he had won for his country at Appomattox in 1865 would endure. When Grant died of cancer twenty years later in 1885, at the age of 63, he asked that the pallbearers at his funeral be composed of an equal mix of former Union and Confederate generals. The words still inscribed today over his tomb are the same words he adopted as a campaign slogan in his first presidential race: Let Us Have Peace.

**Other great books by Michael W. Simmons on Kindle, paperback and audio:**

Elizabeth I: Legendary Queen Of England

Alexander Hamilton: First Architect Of The American Government

William Shakespeare: An Intimate Look Into The Life Of The Most Brilliant Writer In The History Of The English Language

Thomas Edison: American Inventor

Catherine the Great: Last Empress of Russia

Romanov: The Last Tsarist Dynasty

Peter the Great: Autocrat and Reformer

The Rothschilds: The Dynasty and the Legacy

Queen Victoria: Icon of an Era

Six Wives: The Women Who Married, Lived, and
Died for Henry VIII

John D. Rockefeller: The Wealthiest Man in
American History

Princess to Queen: The Early Years of Queen
Elizabeth II

Queen of People's Hearts: The Life and Mission
of Diana, Princess of Wales

# Jackie Kennedy Onassis: The Widow of Camelot

Made in the USA
Middletown, DE
31 March 2019